THE COMPLETE BEGINNERS GUIDE TO SEED SAVING

A HASSLE-FREE JOURNEY TO SELF-SUFFICIENCY, SUSTAINABILITY AND BIODIVERSITY IN YOUR GARDEN

P. JOSEPH RICHARDS

TABLE OF CONTENTS

INTRODUCTION

In 1903, you would've had just under 500 varieties of lettuce plants to choose from, but by 1983, that number had depleted to 36. In general, we've lost about 93% of our unique seed strands just in the 20th century (Fast Company, 2012). Unless we step in and reverse this trend, that's just a glimpse of what we can expect going forward.

But first, why is this depletion happening? Well, genetic modification. It's the squash that can withstand a drought and whose seeds will sowed next season. The most enormous, sweetest watermelon seeds survive, while the rest aren't worth keeping. The sweet corn that produces four times as much come harvest time will move up the priority list of preferred crops to replant for next year.

We want the best results for our time and effort. However, there's power in numbers, and nature prefers diversity—that's how we've all survived this long in the first place. We can look at the human gene pool and see that more diversity is beneficial in preventing autoimmune diseases or fatal genetic mutations. We can also look at monocultures—how they strip the soil and require more intricate care to keep alive—and see that *this* method isn't sustainable. We can acknowledge that we can't bend nature to our will without severe consequences. We can look at nature's most steadfast rule, "survival of the fittest," and deduce that the strongest, fastest, most resilient life forms result from biodiversity, not despite it.

You've decided you want to get your hands dirty (literally) and start your garden. Whatever pushed you toward growing your food, whether it's the cost-of-living crisis or the eco-sustainability movement, it doesn't make sense if you still depend on buying your seeds in the store. The costs of buying seeds, seedlings, and whole plants, in addition to all the other expenses and resources that go into a healthy garden, quickly add up and become unaffordable and unrealistic.

Being raised on a farm with implementations of permaculture principles (living off the land sustainably, composting, working with nature instead of against it, and, of course, seed saving), you quickly learn that it is truly the best way to live, not only for us in the present and future but for the environment. Did I have my doubts? Did I complain about some of the "luxuries" I missed out on as a grumpy teen? You bet!

But the older I got, the more I started appreciating nature and experiencing every consequence our actions have on the land. We get so caught up in things that don't matter that we don't realize we're neglecting (and, in most cases, ruining) the one thing that continues to give us life. At one point, I could think about one question day and night: *How much more are we going to take, and how much longer is nature willing to give?*

That's my origin story in a nutshell. It started with adapting our farm to be even more eco-conscious and sustainable. I didn't expect it would grow into a deep-rooted (excuse the pun) passion of wanting to teach others that it's possible to make a difference, even on a small scale. We can take care of this floating space rock so it can keep on giving back to us for generations to come.

But learning wasn't without its challenges. The more I researched, the more I became aware of everything I didn't know yet or hadn't even considered. It's overwhelming. However, the Dunning-Kruger effect wouldn't stop me from going on my journey. The Dunning-Kruger effect is a cognitive bias that suggests that the more you learn about a particular subject, the more you will doubt your knowledge, competence, or capabilities.

Think of learning everything there is to know about a subject. It is like an ice cube in water, with only 10% showing above the surface. Many people will stop at 10% and be done (and wildly overestimate their knowledge), but the deeper you go, the more there is to discover, making you doubt your ability to learn and retain the other 90%.

I'm glad I didn't let the mental barrier of having a lack of knowledge stop me. I have never felt more content than when strolling through the farm and being present in the ever-giving haven we built with our hands. It took me years to learn as much as I know now, and I still don't quite understand everything. But what got me this far is my willingness to learn and to do it one step at a time.

When you start or manage your garden, you will undoubtedly be faced with obstacles (some worse than others), such as pest and disease management without depending on chemical fertilizers, limited garden space (because who can afford to own land these days?), unpredictable weather and seasonal changes, on top of an already busy lifestyle. But here's the thing: permaculture makes gardening more manageable, not harder. So, if you have a garden and want to implement permaculture gardening, I have a handbook dedicated to what it is and how to do it.

If you want to be at the forefront of the sustainability and eco-conscious movement, name a better place to start than an in-depth guide on how to save seeds—and potentially save the dwindling numbers of unique strands of fruits and vegetable varieties in the process. It all starts with gathering the knowledge, absorbing it, practicing it, and not being afraid of failing or making mistakes (and learning from them).

My background taught me how vital seed saving is in permaculture gardening practices. Additionally, knowing how to save seeds to remain stable and viable for as long as possible is crucial. Whether you're a complete beginner or already have a thriving food forest, it's always early enough to learn the value of seed-saving and how it can promote biodiversity, improve food security, and leave you feeling fulfilled by your role.

As you learn various seed-saving techniques, drastically reduce your reliance on store-bought seeds and seedlings, and improve your gardening practices, you will gain the confidence to take your backyard garden to a new level. No contribution to increasing the number of plant varieties and biodiversity is too insignificant.

By the end of this book, you will have all the knowledge you need to step forth and cultivate a diverse and resilient garden from the seeds you save and grow yourself in perpetuity. It's a closed circle of resilience and self-reliance.

You'll save money and life's most precious resource—time. You'll wake up one day and realize you've become that person. You know? The person you've always wanted to become: self-sufficient, knowledgeable, resourceful, eco-conscious, and with a garden that thanks you in abundance.

1

SEED SAVING BASICS

C onsider that a single tomato has, on average, between 150 and 300 seeds inside it. That's one tomato with the potential to grow more than 100 other plants. But what do you do with so many seeds? And how do you store them?

Slow down—this guide will answer all your questions in good time. In this chapter, we'll go over the basics of seed saving, why you should do it, and what you should consider first and foremost.

WHAT IS SEED SAVING?

As the name suggests, seed saving (also known as brown bagging) is the act of saving seeds to plant them again or to increase the number of plants you have (and therefore increase your yield). Saving seeds also involves storing other reproductive material from fruits, vegetables, grain, herbs, and flowering plants (cuttings, tubers, roots, etc.).

The seed-saving process is more nuanced than just putting seeds in a plastic jar. We want the best possible harvest next year—

because why wouldn't we? So, you select the best plants—the ones that are the most healthy and resilient. Then, you collect seeds from various produce of the same type (not just from one plant). You then need to process and store the seeds correctly to use them the next time you want to plant them.

The main objectives of seed saving are to preserve heirloom seeds (which we will discuss thoroughly in the next chapter), preserve open-pollinated seed varieties (diversity within the genetics), encourage self-reliance, and save rare or endangered plant species from looming extinction.

A BRIEF HISTORY LESSON

Seed saving has been traced back as far as 30,000 years ago (Allaby et al., 2017). Granted, back then, we humans were still mainly reliant on hunting and gathering our food rather than farming it. Evidence suggests that crop cultivation started roughly 11,000 years ago; at around the same time, the domestication of cattle and various other farm animals became all the rage. You know what they say: work smarter, not harder.

The exact reason why farming and seed saving became the logical thing to do isn't known, but it's likely due to a variety of factors: the climate shifted, which led to a decline in food sources and availability, animals migrated, and steady human population growth didn't exactly help. At the same time, the new climate brought about the perfect conditions for annual vegetation. With some observation, they likely started to recreate the conditions under which crops grew. They could successfully own wheat, rice, corn, fruits, and vegetable fields with some practice and even keep animals for meat.

One thing is sure. Farming was necessary for survival for a long time, so people had to figure it out. So what happened? Why is no one growing their food and saving seeds anymore?

The answer is, of course, capitalism, consumerism, and corporate control. After the colonization of America, Europeans ran into some issues when the seeds they brought from the other side of the world failed to grow or produce a sufficient yield. In light of this problem, the US formed a patent office for agriculture. 1862, the United States Department of Agriculture (USDA) was born. Their plan was simple and effective: hand out free seeds to farmers to grow and adapt to different climates so there's more food.

Private sectors thought this solution was a waste of a great opportunity, and in 1883, the American Seed Trade Association (ASTA) was established. Less than 50 years later, ASTA convinced the government to stop this nonsense—no more free seeds for anyone. To add insult to injury, ASTA also developed and implemented intellectual property rights and patents that made it illegal to save seeds that belonged to these private corporations.

Mega agricultural corporations own over 67% of seeds worldwide as of right now. Any seeds you buy at the garden store are held and patented. Not only that, but they're also most likely treated with harsh chemicals and genetically modified to depend on pesticides (regardless of what the packaging says).

That is how you kill over 11,000 years of history and life-giving tradition in less than a decade. Today, home gardeners do most of the seed saving and what's left of the nomadic tribes in some parts of the world.

TYPES OF SEEDS

Knowledge is indeed power, and before you go and start gathering seeds, there are a few things you need to know. There are three main types of seeds: open-pollinated, hybrid, and GMO. Each type has its benefits and drawbacks, and the seed you choose to grow and save will depend on your specific needs and goals.

Open-Pollinated Seeds

When a plant or flower is fertilized through natural means by insects, birds, rain, and wind by a plant of the same variety, the seed is genetically similar to its "parents" with only slight variations. These variations in the genetic makeup of the seed offspring are how plants gradually adapt to environmental changes.

Keep open-pollinated seeds separate from other varieties of the same family or genus. Otherwise, cross-pollination between two variants of the same plant species can happen naturally, so you will no longer have open-pollinated (or heirloom) seeds but hybrids.

Hybrid Seeds

Hybrid seeds are when two varieties of plants cross-pollinate (organically or manually), resulting in seeds with a much more diverse genetic makeup. For example, suppose you fertilize a disease-resistant tomato plant with a drought-resistant tomato plant of a different variety, and you continue to save and plant these seeds. In that case, you will eventually end up with seeds with positive characteristics of both varieties (a disease- and drought-resistant tomato plant). This process is a form of genetic engineering and modification.

However, the seeds you get from crossing two different crop varieties are highly unpredictable, and, in many cases, they're not even viable (because they're infertile) and won't germinate or survive for very long. But even if you manage to get past all that, this new variation of the plant you created will only be stable and predictable for a very short time. You need to know what you're doing if you want to make an entirely new species of crop.

GMO Seeds

As I'm sure you're familiar with, GMO stands for Genetically Modified Organism. But unlike hybrid seeds, where cross-pollination is still somewhat natural, GMO seeds are made in a controlled environment (a laboratory), involve expensive and complex technology and engineering, and utilize gene splicing (the stuff you read about in sci-fi novels). These seeds are most commonly made for large-scale commercial use only since you need a license to grow these "Frankensteined" seeds. The seeds you buy at the store are not this modified, but they might still be hybrids.

Heirloom Seeds

Heirloom seeds aren't a type of seed on their own, but it's worth mentioning what they are and how they come to be. Almost any seed can be an heirloom seed. The category means that the seed has a long history of being open-pollinated. An heirloom seed, through years of cultivation (a minimum of 50 generations), likely has had many desirable traits passed down to it, such as hardiness, better nutritional value, flavor, productivity, and resistance to pests and diseases. It's also perfectly adapted to the climate it's in.

THE SEED-SAVING CYCLE

In gardening, both heirloom and hybrid seeds have their place. Heirloom seeds ensure that every generation of seeds results in better-quality plants—the genes both improve and get "solidified," meaning that the chances of it failing for any reason and going extinct are less, and we get better quality food from them. Hybrid seeds ensure a more extensive variety of species to choose from, grow, and enjoy.

However, cross-pollination is only sometimes successful, especially if you let it happen naturally. If you want to create a stable hybrid variety, you will likely run into some issues in the future. But it *is* doable.

Before starting your seed-saving journey, you must know how the cycle goes. Some of it is self-explanatory, but some involve nuance and many things to remember—as you'll see.

Planting

Whether you already have a thriving garden or are just starting, the first step is to have or grow healthy, open-pollinated plants. Ensure that plants of the same species or varieties are isolated in some way so they don't cross-pollinate when the time comes. You also want to ensure that you're providing the proper care to your plants and garden regarding water, soil quality, and sun requirements.

Pollination

As mentioned, you want only to create and harvest hybrid seeds if you already have hybrid plants that made it through the first generation of replanting. However, even with hybrid plants, you want to ensure pollination by other plants with the same genetic variety. In short, don't breed two different types of hybrid plants.

Remember that some plants are self-pollinating and will pollinate themselves before the flowers open up. However, self-pollinating plants are not immune to cross-pollination, as insects can still crawl into the flowers and pollinate them. You need to know which plants are more likely to cross-pollinate and which aren't so you can take the necessary precautions to minimize the possibility (which we will discuss later).

Seed Maturity

The produce is often ready for picking and eating long before the seed matures. It's essential to allow the seed to develop and grow on the plant before it gets harvested. Do some research on the plants in your garden to ensure you're not picking the produce and saving underdeveloped seeds.

Underdeveloped seeds can still germinate. However, they might be weak and end up not surviving for very long, unable to withstand harsh weather, and producing a small or underperforming yield.

You should always leave a few fruits or vegetables on the plant until the seed has fully matured before picking them and moving on to the next step.

Harvesting

Crops can either be dry-fruited or wet-fruited. It's pretty simple to distinguish between these two types of seed: if the seed is inside the fruit, it's wet-seeded (tomatoes, squash, watermelon, peppers, etc.), and if it's not inside a fruit, it's dry seed (usually inside a pod, tract, capsule, or seed head).

The fruit has to be fully ripe or overripe with wet seeds to ensure they are mature before you can harvest and process them for storage. Dry seeds should remain on the plant until they're mature enough (you can look up what color or texture dry seeds from specific crops should look like when matured) before harvesting and storing them.

Processing

Wet seeds often have pieces of fruit pulp or jelly stuck to or surrounding them (like tomato seeds surrounded by a jelly-like sac). Even dry seeds might have some moisture even when they're mature and the seed head is wholly dried out. For this reason, you should always ensure the seeds are sufficiently dried if you want to save them for long periods (otherwise, they might sprout prematurely or decay).

For wet seeds with lots of pulp or jelly sacks surrounding them, there are several ways to make separating them more manageable. You can put the seeds in a container and place them in a dark but warm environment away from sunlight so they can ferment. After a few days, mold will form on top. At this point, you can add water and, with gloves on, squish everything together so the seeds get released from the pulp or goo surrounding it. The moldy pulp or jelly will float to the surface while the seeds fall to the bottom. This process makes it easier to separate the jelly bits from the seeds by scooping out (or pouring off) the top layer of gunk.

From here, you can strain, rinse, and dry the seeds. For dry seeds (after you've separated them from seed pods and plant debris), you can spread them thinly on trays and leave them to dry. The drying process for wet-fruited and dry-fruited seeds can take up to three weeks.

Storage

Seeds processed and dried can be stored in airtight containers in a cool, dark, dry place such as a closet or basement for up to a year or two. For several years, you can keep the seeds in airtight containers in the fridge or freezer. However, some seeds are notoriously known to have a shorter "shelf life" and won't last as long, so be sure to use them before they "expire."

Always label your seed containers with the crop type, variety name, date of harvest, and any other information that might be useful, such as how long you can store the seeds or how many plants you harvested from.

THE BENEFITS OF SEED SAVING

Many traditions don't serve the human race. Throwing them away would benefit society immensely—like consumerism and sketchy marketing strategies. But seed saving has so many benefits that it's hard not to consider doing it.

It would be best if you honored this significant old tradition for the following reasons:

- It's free.
- It's relatively easy after learning the basics.
- It results in more resilient and bountiful crops every year.
- It results in better produce every year.
- Home-saved seeds have higher germination rates.
- You're contributing to your independence instead of capitalism.
- You are contributing toward and improving genetic diversity.
- You're in control of your food supply.

- You learn a valuable and essential skill.
- Eventually, you have heirloom seeds to pass on to the next generation.

CHALLENGES FACING THE SEED-SAVING MOVEMENT

The number one problem the seed-saving movement is trying to solve is the need for more diversity regarding the rate at which fruit and vegetable varieties are declining. Seed Savers Exchange (SSE), a non-profit organization in Iowa, has done a fantastic job preserving these dwindling statistics by growing their vegetable seed bank to over 20,000 varieties.

With the economy hanging on by a thread, more people are now turning to grow their food out of desperation. Of course, this process highlighted how much control big corporations have over the seed industry and the legal implications on the public's ability to save and share seeds.

The seed-saving movement has gained much traction, but it's still mainly comprised of small players (such as school and home gardens, a handful of small-scale commercial farms, and a few non-profits). This fact means that funding and resources are limited.

And since seed saving isn't a common tradition anymore, the lack of knowledge breeds doubt, uncertainty, and apprehension in even the keenest gardeners. Moreover, urbanization led to a significant loss of space to grow enough food to feed a family, and 40-hour work weeks leave us exhausted. So many people who want to join this movement need to learn how, don't have the space, and need more time or energy to do much of anything. Even when working themselves into the ground, many people need more financial wiggle room to donate to the cause.

But an even bigger issue that the seed-saving movement—and most of us—is trying to outrun is the adverse effects of climate change. While politicians debate whether it's real, the people growing our food must deal with the ever-growing proof (and threat) of its existence.

Don't fret. The seed-saving movement has been steadily growing for many years, and although the movement spent many of those years growing in silence, there will be a storm. Mark my words.

SEED SAVING MYTHS AND MISCONCEPTIONS

Seed saving has existed longer than we can conceptualize. However, our ancestors went through much trial and error to learn how to do it properly. Based on them passing on their hard-earned information and knowledge, we have the luxury of buying and reading books about it and looking it up on Google.

However, there's also a lot of misinformation about seed saving out there—some of which might've even played a role in your ambivalence. Let's clear up some of the most common myths and misconceptions about seed saving right now:

You Don't Need Any Special Knowledge

While seed saving is more complicated than you might think, it's not common knowledge either. There is a lot of information, and there are a lot of things to remember. For example, different seeds require different processing and storage needs. Some plants are more likely to cross-pollinate than others, and so on. It's more than just bottling up some seeds; you must know its specifics. But it's completely doable.

Heirlooms Are Always Best

This statement is only sometimes true. Some heirlooms have a shorter shelf-life and require more specialized care than hybrids. This fact is especially true for heirlooms that cultivate asexually (they grow a new plant from a fragment of the mother plant), meaning they are genetically identical to their parent, which increases their risk of infection and disease.

All Seeds Can Be Saved

Within each plant's genetic makeup, there are beneficial and harmful traits that survive to the next generation. Valuable traits are usually dominant, meaning the chances of getting a diseased or mutated plant are less, but it still happens. Diseased, weak, or mutated plants need to be "thinned out" (in other words, removed and preferably composted) with every new generation without saving the seeds; otherwise, you risk these traits surviving.

You Must Isolate All Crop Varieties

It depends on your goals, honestly. If you plan on selling or sharing seeds, you must avoid cross-pollination. If you're creating your variety of fruit or vegetable, and that variety's existence depends entirely on you, then you should also be careful that the "bloodline" is not contaminated. But if you have a decently sized seed bank and you're not too concerned with cross-pollination in your backyard, you can afford to take the risk (you might even end up with an improved variety).

It Takes No Extra Effort

Hey! I said it wasn't that difficult, not that it doesn't take time and effort. Of course, picking, cleaning, processing, labeling, and storing the seeds take time. And then there's a certain amount of time you'll spend researching, gaining practical experience, and learning from mistakes. You'll need to know how to tell which plants are the best from a genetic standpoint (it's not only about the size of the fruit or how much the plant produces) and many other factors that go into seed saving. But it's a necessary learning curve. I call it school fees—the price you pay for knowledge.

SOMETHING TO CONSIDER

To determine whether seed saving is your practice, reflect on your gardening goals for a few minutes. Ask yourself why you started gardening in the first place and how saving and using your seeds could contribute to those goals.

Is the goal to become more self-sufficient or eco-conscious, save money on groceries, and have fresh herbs to supplement your cooking, or is it more of an eccentric hobby now? Or do you have a different goal in mind? Remember, even if you're not yet sharpening your shovel to join the seed-saving movement, saving and using your home garden's seeds can still benefit you on a personal, small-scale level (as well as the environment in the long term).

Now that you know the history and bare basics of seed saving, what it entails, the types of seeds and how they come about, and the impact your seed-saving journey can have on the environment, we will use this information moving forward. In the next chapter, we'll discuss heirloom seeds and their importance.

2

WHY HEIRLOOM SEEDS MATTER

H eirloom seeds are the antique furniture of the gardening world. In the previous chapter, we mentioned that heirloom seeds can be finicky and don't always result in the most resilient plants, but they're still important for many reasons. And just like baggy jeans, they're making a comeback!

DEFINE HEIRLOOM

Heirloom plants (also known as heirloom varieties or heritage plants) are plants grown and maintained by gardeners and farmers (usually in isolated communities) for generations via open pollination. This process isolates them to prevent cross-pollination, and every time the plant leaves behind seeds, those seeds are saved and used in the next growing season. However, heritage plants can also be cultivated and maintained through grafts and cuttings.

For a plant to be considered an heirloom plant, the specific variety of plant needs to be at least 50 years old. Heirloom seeds usually have apparent, desirable traits that have been passed down and reinforced. A plant doesn't just survive that long without picking up some superhuman (or "super-plant") genetics. But again, this concept doesn't mean they can't or don't put out some less-than-optimal seeds now and then.

The bottom line is that heirloom seeds are old, open-pollinated, non-hybrid, and something so valuable that they get passed on to the next generation of trustworthy gardeners. They're a big reason why we had so many varieties of fruits and vegetables to choose from in the past.

However, it's more than the age, rarity, and exceptional genetics that make these seeds so unique. It's the culture surrounding them as well, the stories they carry with them, and their uniqueness that adds to their inherent value and importance.

Their Significance

While hybrid seeds play a significant role in expanding variety and genetic diversity, it's always a gamble; crossing two varieties of corn will result in offspring that have a genetic mix of the two plant parents, but there's no telling what would happen if you save those hybrid seeds and plant them next season. Will you get the same results in the second generation as in the first? You'll end up with infertile seed at worst and diminished returns at best.

This information means that if you plan on creating a variety of your own through cross-pollination, you shouldn't count on these plants to feed you and your family. It also means that if you want to play mad scientist and recreate your original results (because you liked the resulting fruit or vegetables and want another successful yield), you must cross the original two varieties repeatedly from scratch or keep buying hybrid seeds yearly. You can only save hybrid seeds once the genes become stable (meaning the resulting plants and produce of hybrid seeds no longer have any outliers when replanted), which takes an immense amount of time and patience.

Heirloom seeds ensure that variety survives the test of time, and they grow stronger with each generation because they acquire natural resistance to pests, diseases, and climate changes. Heirloom seeds always produce fruit and vegetables that are true to type. Hence, the tomato you pick today from a heritage (or heirloom) plant has the same genetic code that your great-grandma harvested before World War II (give or take a few beneficial mutations as it continually adapts to the environment). We can save the seeds of an heirloom without fear of unpredictable results. And that's why they're so important: preservation of species.

All this talk is about preserving biodiversity, but why is preserving biodiversity so essential? Well, when you only focus on cultivating one variety of fruit and vegetables and have fields upon fields of the same crop type, it only takes a little to destroy an entire harvest and wipe out a whole country's food supply. For example, the Irish potato famine led to the death of a million people because their primary food source was compromised. They grew one variety of potatoes (Irish Lumpers), and the yield succumbed to a blight.

That's the problem with putting all your eggs in one basket; it topples easily and leaves you with no backup plan.

FINDING AND SELECTING HEIRLOOM SEEDS

Heirloom seeds are known because they taste better, have better nutritional value, and are hardy. And yes, buying heirloom seeds to fill up your entire garden can be expensive (unless you inherited some from your parents or grandparents). Still, if having heirloom varieties in your garden is something you want, the investment is worth it.

You can get heirloom seeds or even seedlings from your area if you have reputable garden stores. But research where they get their seeds and ensure they're chemical-free. Also, farmer's markets, garden centers, and seed swap communities are all fantastic options for sourcing heirloom seeds.

Getting seeds in or around your area (non-commercially) is the best-case scenario since that's your best chance to ensure the seeds (or seedlings) are locally sourced and grown. Plus, they've adapted to the climate you reside in.

Otherwise, you can order the heirloom seeds online or through catalogs. Just do your research and make sure whatever website you buy them from is legitimate. Here are a few examples of trust-worthy websites that sell quality heirloom seeds at great prices:

- True Leaf Market
- Baker Creek Heirloom Seeds
- Seed Savers Exchange
- Eden Brothers
- Select Seeds

You should do extensive research and decide beforehand what type of heirloom fruits and veggies you want to grow, how many varieties you want, and their requirements and maturing times.

Don't be afraid to experiment with unique varieties—did you know there's a variety of purple tomatoes? No one said gardening has to be boring. I encourage you to go after unconventional fruit and vegetable varieties since this choice will do even more to preserve genetic diversity.

Now you know where to find heirloom seeds, but what do you look for or consider when selecting them? Besides looking for the word "heirloom" or the abbreviation OP, which stands for open-pollinated (which may not be heirloom at the time of purchase, but they *can* eventually become heirloom in your garden), most of it is personal preference. However, some limitations might prevent you from growing your desired plants. The space you have available, the amount of sunlight your garden gets, your specific climate, and existing companion guilds that might be negatively impacted by certain plants will shorten your choices for heirlooms.

The most crucial factor is whether the seed will fit your needs or goals. Don't plant something you don't want or that doesn't benefit you or your garden.

A pro tip: don't wait until spring is knocking on your door to purchase heirloom seeds because the best varieties sell out quickly, and if you wait until May, you might miss out on the ones you had in mind. You can stock up on seeds months or years in advance if you store them properly.

To store your purchased heirloom seeds, you can remove them from the original packaging and place them in an air-tight container with a packet of silica gel (which will absorb any moisture). Keep the container in a cool, dark place or the freezer for long-term storage. Label them with the proper information (year collected, date stored, and variety).

GROWING HEIRLOOM PLANTS

For the most part, growing heirloom plants are like growing any other plant. The requirements are typically the same. The only difference is you will get attached to your heirlooms—of all your plants in your garden, you don't want your heirlooms to die.

As mentioned before, you need to choose the variety of heirloom vegetables carefully based on the climate you're in and the conditions of your garden. Know your soil type and quality (or grow your heirlooms in containers or raised garden beds so you have complete control over this aspect), and consider the unique or beneficial traits you need or want and research which variety has them (hint: pick those!).

Remember that no plant (no matter its lineage) is resistant to all diseases. You still need to practice good gardening hygiene, crop rotation, soil management, and cover cropping to prevent diseases from wreaking havoc on or destroying all of your hard work.

Using organic mulch (and fertilizer) and knowing how to water your garden correctly and consistently will prevent fungal diseases, root rot, and a host of other issues from occurring. Supporting your plants with stakes or trellises where necessary is also a good idea. Furthermore, you should monitor your plants regularly for pests and signs of potential health problems and deal with them before they spread or kill the plant. The best cure for diseases or pests is prevention, and you can do this by using pest-repellent plants or other natural methods.

If you find dead or diseased plants, remove them immediately and sterilize all your garden tools. Overcrowding your garden will also contribute to diseases and pests and might cause plants to under-produce and die. Stick to the recommended spacing distances and bear in mind the root systems of your crops.

Some garden produce (like lettuce, spinach, and other tender crops) are best eaten shortly after harvesting. Please feel free to harvest all fruits and vegetables at once; instead, harvest and use or eat them as needed. This method is also why you should space out germination and planting (succession planting) so that everything isn't ripe and ready for picking simultaneously.

Allow the produce to ripen before you pick them to ensure you get the best flavor. Remember to allow some fruit and vegetables from different (healthy) plants to become overripe on the plant so you can save those seeds for next year!

HEIRLOOMS AND COMMUNITY

What do you get when people with similar goals come together? A community. Seed saving doesn't have to be something you do alone. It's far more fulfilling and helpful if you do it in unity as part of a much larger circle of passionate individuals.

Before people bought seeds in supermarkets, they were traded and swapped between communities and neighbors. Keeping that sense of community alive is essential, not only because it brings people together but also because it keeps the practice alive. It circulates the knowledge of how to do it so future generations can continue the legacy of saving seeds. It enables local gardeners and smaller agricultural centers to swap seeds instead of buying them.

Seed saving, swapping, and passing down heirloom seeds to your children keep the culture alive and enrich the stories connected to these seeds. Even if you're not interested in a seed that dates back to the 1800s, you must admit it's pretty cool to think about every-thing this plant's lineage has been through, the different hills and backyards it grew on, and what it survived. If only plants could talk!

And you can be part of that history, too. You can become part of a community that helps and supports one another in a collective mission, even if your main goal is to have great-tasting (or interesting-looking) lettuce and tomatoes for your garden salad.

REMEMBER

Your gardening objective is unique to you. No rule says you need to grow heirlooms, but you have to admit the benefits of doing so are undeniable. You get to help the environment, preserve the variety for future generations, and enjoy superior quality fruits and vegetables. You become part of the already rich history and can pass the seeds down and tell the stories to your children or grandchildren.

Heirlooms are an essential aspect of gardening. In a way, it's less effort than buying and growing hybrid seeds every year because you can save the seeds, swap or sell them, or expand your garden when you're ready and able to do so.

In either event, there's a lot more to saving seeds and how to do it properly so you don't risk the integrity of (or accidentally killing) the seed. In the next chapter, we will detail how to store seeds for both the short and long term.

3

SEED PRESERVATION 101

At the risk of sounding a bit dramatic, seed saving is like preserving or capturing time in a bottle to experience in the future. But if you're going to do it, it needs to be done correctly. In this chapter, we go into more detail about storing seeds, including why it's important, the different methods, testing viability, tools you'll need, how to avoid common mistakes, and more.

WHY PRESERVATION IS KEY

To a gardener, nothing is quite as fulfilling as raising a plant from a seed into a thriving and bountiful plant. To continue that lineage with every passing year, they hold a very high regard. It is indeed something to be proud of.

Without the seed, we have no harvest to enjoy. Saving seeds is a way to honor the hard work and dedication of our predecessors in addition to feeding our bodies. It's a commitment to carry on their legacy because a gardener's impact lives on with every passing generation.

Another, and perhaps more important, reason why the preservation of seeds is essential is what's known as "domestication." Over the millennia, we've turned plants that were once able to thrive in the wild into plants utterly dependent on us for survival. For example, sweeter and larger fruit-bearing plants survived over plants that could withstand harsh climates. Resilience was less important than a bigger harvest.

Nowadays, domesticated plants can't survive without constant pruning, weeding, and irrigation because that's what we agreed to provide them with thousands of years ago. From a permaculture point of view, seed saving is non-negotiable since the goal is to work with nature instead of against it and to reduce our negative impact on the ecosystem. But we must recognize that it must make sense financially and for personal gain.

Preserving your seeds is an assurance policy. Sometimes, certain seed varieties are in short supply because big corporations corner the market and condense the supply or availability of some varieties (they only keep the most profitable seeds around, and each year, more and more unique varieties are discontinued or aren't worth restocking). Saving and preserving your seeds gives you more control of your supply and varieties and allows you to swap with others.

Preserving your seeds also means you have more control over the quality and quantity of seeds you have at no additional cost. Most importantly, you can decide which seeds to save based on selective breeding and superior traits. Your garden will be stronger and better with each generation of seeds you save.

METHODS OF PRESERVATION

If you're starting with saving your seeds, start conservatively (with only one or two types of crops) and with self-pollinating varieties since they are more likely to bear open-pollinated (or "true to type") seeds instead of hybrid seeds. As for what comes after, here's what you should know.

Cleaning Seeds

Once you've harvested the seeds, you must immediately clean them to remove dirt, dust, and soil residue. You can use a clean, damp towel. Some seeds will require you first to remove seed coatings, shells, husks, pods, gel sacs, pulp, or other forms of plant matter and debris. You can usually use your hands, fingernails, or tweezers.

You need to ensure you know the proper way to clean and process the seeds you have before moving on to drying them.

Drying Seeds

Spread your now clean seeds thinly onto trays (or plates), which you can line with dye-free paper towels, wax paper, parchment paper, or a screen or mesh. Don't use newspaper, as the ink might seep into the seed, reducing its viability or germination rate. Some people use ovens or food dehydrators set to the lowest heat to speed up drying, but this method can potentially damage the seed.

Ventilation and air movement are the safest and most convenient ways to dry your seeds. Stirring the seeds now and then (even if they're spread thinly on the trays) ensures that all the seeds—and all sides of all the seeds—receive thorough ventilation so they dry evenly. If you live in an area where it rains frequently or is always humid, having the seeds stay in front of (or even just in the same room as) an electric fan will prevent them from taking too long to dry (and either growing mold or accidentally germinating).

The optimal moisture content in seeds for storage is between 5% and 10%. However, since the typical home gardener will need more resources or tools to measure this percentage, it usually takes one to three weeks. You'll know when the seeds are properly dried when they're hard and don't give when squeezing them, bend, or leave an indent when pressing your fingernail into them (this test is called the fingernail test).

Controlling and Monitoring Storage Conditions

During seed storage, you must avoid four things: moisture, air, warmth, and light. Humidity and warmth can both result in rehydration of the seed (causing mold or bacteria growth or premature germination in storage). In contrast, air and light will cause the seed to deteriorate quickly ("expire" or lose viability sooner than usual).

Seeds do best when stored between 32°F and 50°F, but it's even more important to keep the temperatures as constant as possible (no sudden temperature spikes or drops). If you're storing them in fridges or freezers, they should be in ones that aren't going to open regularly.

Furthermore, it would be best to store seeds in air-tight packaging (such as opaque plastic or glass jars, resealable plastic bags, aluminum foil packets, or paper envelopes) away from sunlight. Additionally, you can make use of silica gel, charcoal, or rice to minimize and control the humidity levels inside the containers, as well as cushioning material (crumpled-up paper towels or cloth) so the seeds don't get damaged by smacking into each other or the sides of the container.

Short or Long Term Solutions

For short-term storage (less than two or three years), you can keep the seed containers refrigerated or in a dark, cool cupboard or closet if you live in a cooler climate. You may freeze them for long-term storage (more than three years). If you plan on storing the seeds for over three years, consider investing in a vacuum sealer to seal your seeds before freezing. Remember to label them appropriately.

Storing your seeds in a fridge or freezer is unnecessary, but it helps keep the conditions consistent when your climate is unpredictable. Not to mention, bacteria and mold are much less likely to grow on your seeds if you store them in the fridge or freezer. As long as your seeds are thoroughly and properly dried and in airtight containers, they only stand to benefit from this storage method.

You'll also want to check in on your storage environment now and then (once or twice a month at least) to ensure the containers or bags are still intact, no light is getting to them, and the temperature and other storage factors are staying consistent.

Monitor Viability

It's essential to keep in mind that some seeds have a very short life expectancy or "shelf-life," meaning they can only be stored for a few months at most before they deteriorate (examples of seeds with short expiration dates include chives, onions, garlic, leeks, parsnips, and turnips). However, when stored properly, most seeds have three to five years of shelf life.

Seeds with a medium to extended life expectancy, like brassicas, cucumber, tomatoes, melons, and pumpkin, can be stored for up to five years. However, germination rates will naturally decline the longer they are stored, so you should test the viability of these seeds every year. You do this by taking a sample of seeds (a minimum of 10) out of storage, letting them come to room temperature, and rehydrating them. An effective way to rehydrate your seeds is to soak them in water overnight before placing them between a folded paper towel (to keep them moist). Then, place the paper towel in a Ziploc bag and leave it somewhere humid (I find the kitchen works well for this process).

To avoid having to remove an entire container of seeds from their proper storage conditions (and potentially contaminating them by opening up the container and exposing them to humidity or pathogens) to acquire a sample, you can isolate and sort all seeds into groups of ten by using smaller Ziploc bags within a more extensive, labeled container.

Using a sample of 10 seeds to test viability makes math simple. Every seed represents 10%. So if, for example, all ten seeds sprout, the germination rate is 100%, but if only four sprouts, it's 40%. As a general rule of thumb, you want to discard stored seeds if the germination rate for that "batch" is lower than 50% since this percentage could indicate the seeds are either too old, have genetic defects, or were stored under improper conditions (which might negatively affect the longevity, production, and hardiness of the plants in that specific group of seeds).

Tools You'll Need

Before you panic and think you'll have to make an expensive trip to the garden store, most of the things you need for harvesting and storing seeds you might already have or will easily be able to substitute or make yourself for way cheaper.

Here's a detailed list of everything you need to harvest, process, and store seeds:

- Blossom bags: Blossom bags are necessary if you're tight on space and need help isolating self-pollinating crop varieties by the appropriate distances. Blossom bags prevent similar crops from cross-pollinating; if you plan to save the seeds, you can't have them cross-pollinating. You can substitute blossom bags for tulle fabric and string or mesh party favor bags (the ones with the drawstrings). You cover the flower before it opens in spring and remove it once the flower petals fall off or you see its setting fruit. Remember that this method only works on plants that self-pollinate (but still risk cross-pollination). You'll have to hand-pollinate plants that require open pollination.
- Tape or ribbon: Use these items to mark fruits that have been hand-pollinated or isolated with blossom bags so you know which fruits (and therefore which seeds) are for sure open-pollinated and will grow back true to type.
- Scissors or pruners: These items are needed to harvest overripe fruit off the plant before processing the seeds. Some fruits or flowers might have no problem parting with their mothers with a gentle tug; however, you can damage the plant if you have to put some force into every fruit or flower you harvest.
- Gloves, knives, and tweezers: You might have to remove seeds from inside fruit, husks, pods, or shells after they dry. Gloves prevent you from getting cuts or splinters when cracking open dried seed coverings, the knife is for cutting

fruit to get to the seed inside, and you can use tweezers for many functions (such as organizing or planting tiny seeds or seedlings and removing plant matter that's stuck to the seeds).

- Cloth: Use a cloth to clean the seeds. A wipe-down is typically sufficient for cleaning seeds in flower heads or pods.

- Containers: Mason jars work perfectly for some seeds that require fermentation before drying, but you can also use old plastic containers. You'll also need containers (glass or plastic jars or sealable plastic bags) that seal air-tight for storing the seeds after drying them. Paper bags also come in handy when extracting seeds from flower heads (this information will make sense later on). Utilize paper envelopes for seeds that aren't going to be stored long-term.

- Trays and liners: Wax or parchment paper works best to prevent seeds from sticking to the tray and aid in helping them dry uniformly. But you can also use paper towels to line the trays (bear in mind the seeds might get stuck to the paper towel, and you'll need to loosen them and replace them once or twice during the drying process). And, of course, you'll need trays for spreading the seeds thinly and evenly. However, you can substitute trays with old, paper, or serving trays you no longer use.

- Labels, pens, or markers: You'll need to label the seed containers with the date harvested, variety, life expectancy, and other helpful information before storage.

- Silica gel packets: This item is one of the very few things on the list that you might have to buy. Silica packets help keep moisture away from stored seeds, preserving them better for extended periods. The great thing about them is they're reusable, so you only need to buy them once. However, you can collect them in other purchases; you can find them in shoes or shoeboxes, medicine bottles, purses, boxes containing electronics, etc. Ask your friends and family if they have any lying around and save them for you.

- Fridge, freezer, or a cool, dark place: You don't have to buy a refrigerator or freezer to use specifically for your seeds, but it does help to think of where you're going to store your seeds so they don't get disturbed too much or risk exposure to something they shouldn't (air, light, moisture, or warmth). This location can be at the back of a cool, dark cupboard or drawer if you live in a colder climate or a separate bar fridge or freezer that you use sparingly.

The following list includes things you don't necessarily need, but that would undoubtedly make your life a whole lot easier, especially if you're processing a lot of seeds for storage:

- Seed sieves or screens: These items will help you separate seeds from foliage, husks, or other types of debris instead of doing it manually (which can be quite labor-intensive and time-consuming if you need to debride hundreds of seeds). However, you can make your seed sieve or screen— there are plenty of resources and step-by-step video guides online. Just calculate the prices of the materials and see whether making one yourself will be more cost-efficient than simply buying one. Also, remember that making one (or investing in a well-made one) will most likely be better quality and last longer than buying an inexpensive one. This decision is totally up to you and what you need.
- Electric fan: Again, unless you're in a warm, humid, or rainy climate, a fan is optional. However, it will decrease the drying time needed and ensure sufficient ventilation. A

fan is a good investment here to speed up the process and leave no room for error (mold or germination).

Seeds well-stored in a garden half-planted. There's nothing quite as demotivating and disappointing as putting all your time and effort into harvesting, processing, and storing your seeds to realize the following year (or the next time you plant them) that none of them are viable anymore—or discovering that your next generation of seeds lost their vigor and aren't growing as fast or producing as much as their predecessors.

THE IMPORTANCE OF PROPER STORAGE

How you store your seeds will affect the seed's genetic integrity, quality, and viability. That's why proper storage conditions for seeds are so vital. It's also an insurance policy. Some leftover seeds from a previous, bountiful season or harvest can supplement a current, underperforming one.

Then there's the fact that you save money because you don't need to keep re-buying seeds every year, and you have a better idea of what to expect from the harvest if you know how the parent plants performed. However, all the benefits of seed storage depend on the seed storage conditions. If you're not vigilant, you risk losing or damaging your entire seed bank.

To reiterate, seeds' germination rate and vigor naturally decline over time, no matter how good your storage conditions are. The point of these rather precise seed storage guidelines is to retain the germination rates of the seeds for as long as possible and to ensure the overall quality of the resulting plant and yield in the future.

There are a few things to keep in mind that will ensure seeds survive both short and long-term storage:

- Mature seeds will retain their viability longer than immature ones will.
- The hard shell or coating of the seed increases the amount of time the seed can last in storage (though probably not far beyond its inherent shelf life).
- The colder the better. It would be best to store seeds in a refrigerator or freezer.
- If a seed is severely damaged before storage (if it's nicked or scratched, for example), it will likely not survive very long. A broken seed is not viable at all.

Containers

The containers you use to store the seeds in have a few straightforward objectives: to keep moisture, light, and pests out and to keep the seeds in. However, the type of container you choose will depend on how long you want to store the seeds. It would be best to use only particular containers for short-term storage; others will keep the seeds safer for longer.

For very short-term storage (a couple of months up to a year, maximum), you can get away with using paper envelopes. For several months and up to two years, Ziploc bags or plastic containers will do great. For multiple years (three or more), glass containers like Mason jars or metal tins work best (as long as they're air-tight).

Optimal Conditions

The conditions for storage help slow the aging process of the seed down. The most crucial factor is that the temperatures shouldn't fluctuate too much or too quickly. Keeping the temperature consistent is more important than keeping it cool. So, a temperature range from 50°F to 60°F is optimal versus a range of 10°F to 40°F.

Recommendations to stick to specific temperature ranges differ depending on your source or who you ask. Still, a general rule of thumb is that the temperature (in Fahrenheit) and the relative humidity shouldn't exceed 100 when combined. For example, if the temperature in storage is 60°F, the humidity levels should be below 40%. However, this rule usually applies if you're storing your seeds under room temperature conditions (in a dark cupboard or drawer).

Additionally, it would be best to keep your seeds dry and away from light.

Cataloging

There is some information regarding your seeds that will come in handy. Adequate labeling and organizing saves more time and effort than it takes to maintain. Therefore, each packet or container of seeds needs a label that contains clear, accurate, relevant, and helpful information to avoid potential identification problems in the future.

The helpful and relevant information might not need to be as detailed as the next seed-saving gardener. It depends on the size and complexity of your garden and what you plan to do with the seeds. What I mean by this information is that a person with a more miniature garden who mainly saves seeds for personal use won't need as detailed labels as someone with a large garden with many varieties and who shares seeds with the community.

With that information in mind, here's all the information you want on your labels whether you're a small or large-scale seed saver:

- Name of the species and variety (or the common name if you don't have many varieties).
- Source: where did you acquire the seed from? Personal garden, store-bought, swapped, etc.
- Harvest date (preferable), received, or bought.

Now, if you do want to add more detail to your labels if only to make your life easier, you can do so by adding some of the following information (if you think it will be helpful) in addition to those mentioned above:

- Short description of the physical or biological characteristics (drought or pest-resistant, for example).
- Requirements (sun, water, soil type preferred, etc.).
- Days to maturity (how long it takes to grow into a mature plant from sowing or germination).
- Germination rate.
- Season or months you should plant them in (and if you should germinate them inside beforehand).
- Number of seeds.

If there are too many seeds to count or tiny seeds, weighing them might help with this step. An easy way is to count out 10-100 (depending on their size) and determine their weight. Use the following formula to determine how many seeds you have:

Even number of seeds = X grams

X grams ÷ specific amount of seeds = weight per seed

Weight of all seeds ÷ weight per seed = total seeds

For example, you count and weigh ten pumpkin seeds. The weight of 10 seeds is 2 g. That means every seed weighs about 0.2 g (2 g ÷ 10 seeds). Now, you weigh all your seeds and divide that by the weight of one seed. Let's say all the pumpkin seeds you have weigh 120 g. 120 g ÷ 0.2 = 600. You have 600 pumpkin seeds in total.

As far as how to organize your seeds, there are a few ways you can sort or catalog them so they're easily accessible and arranged functionally. You can sort them alphabetically by name, type, variety, or planting season.

Sorting seeds alphabetically is the least practical way. But who am I to interfere with your system if it works for you? Alphabetically organizing seeds will require another, more detailed way of keeping track of which seeds need to be taken out of storage and sown at what times. You'll likely need to go through your entire collection every few months to find what you're looking for or need.

Sorting by type or variety isn't that much better, either. Sure, you'll know exactly where to find the broccoli or tomatoes, but it still doesn't provide a straightforward sense of what seeds you need to plant next.

The best way to sort seeds is by planting season. There's an apparent differentiation when spring, summer, and fall crops are separated. For starters, it's a much smaller amount to rummage through for the next season, and you can make it even easier by further organizing each seasonal category.

In other words, you can sort all the seeds for every season so that the seeds that need propagating first are in front. This method requires a lot less additional organization and keeping track of. When you open up your seedbox, fridge, or freezer, keep the seeds that need to be planted or propagated for the next season in the very front.

Also, make a spreadsheet to keep track of your seeds by listing each seed variety, the number of packets you have, how many seeds per packet (and in total), and the year obtained (and prefer-ably month). Any other information that will help you know your seed collection inside and out can also be added, such as "expiry" or sowing dates. Keep the inventory updated whenever you remove or add seeds, and closely monitor the viability dates.

Organizing System

If you're going to put this much love and dedication into some-thing, you have to see it through and do it right from start to finish. Knowing how to set up a well-organized seed storage system that is guaranteed to keep your seeds healthy, safe, and accounted for is just as crucial as preserving them beforehand.

Regarding the organizational side of seed saving, you need to find a system that works for you. Simple and functional are the keywords. It won't benefit you if your system is too time-consuming or expensive to maintain.

Organizing your seeds includes keeping track of your seed inven-tory. You need to know how many types of seeds you have, how many of each variety you have, the harvest date, when you're plan-ning on planting them, and when they need to be used (life expectancy). The goal of your system is to maintain the seeds, planting the oldest seeds first and keeping track of how many seeds you have so you're aware of when it's time for planting again.

This process can be as simple as a notebook and proper labeling. You can also implement strategies like dividing the seeds into cate-gories, using large plastic storage containers (placing new seeds at the bottom and the oldest seeds on top), having a separate holding area for seeds you're planting soon, and notes on crop rotations.

COMMON SEED PRESERVATION PITFALLS

As time passes, you've likely experienced the magic of gardening first-hand. It happens when holding a seedling, harvesting fruit, or simply admiring new growth. You didn't think it was possible to attach this to plants, seedlings, or seeds, but here we are. When you put so much time, energy, and care into your garden, it would be strange not to get attached (even though the average, garden-less person won't understand it).

You've withstood the trials and tribulations of being a beginner gardener, or maybe you're still going through this phase and learning as you go. I want to reassure you that it's okay to make mistakes—overcoming challenges is life's most motivating and educational thing. But it's also perfectly normal and rational to want to avoid running into them. So here are the biggest and most common mistakes people make when starting their seed-saving journey (and how to avoid them):

Saving Hybrid Seeds

Hybrid seeds will most likely either be infertile or result in a mutated plant or produce. Hybrid plants *can* stabilize and result in a new species or variety. Still, this process takes years of adapting, effort, careful selection, and saving seeds over many generations (and failed attempts). Listen, if your life goal is to make a new type of strawberry that's bigger, sweeter, and tie-dyed, don't let me stop you from following your dreams. But the risk and effort aren't worth it if you're gardening to feed yourself or your family.

Not Separating Similar Varieties

You can cross-pollinate plants with similar varieties (in the same family tree). For example, "Sweet Million" and "Sungold" are both varieties of cherry tomatoes. While tomato plants are self-fertile, they can still cross-pollinate if not separated by distance or isolation (blossom bags). You may still get delicious, edible cherry tomatoes, but the resulting fruit will carry hybrid seeds.

Always research the proper isolation distance (which is not 100% fail-safe, by the way) for the varieties you're planning on growing, or take the time to isolate your crops manually—or at least a few flowers on each plant so you can save those seeds without the risk of saving hybrid seeds.

Not Planting Enough of the Same Variety

To preserve genetic diversity and prevent gene bottlenecking, you need to grow enough of the same variety of plants. Otherwise, your plants' genetic stability will eventually deteriorate, resulting in weak, ill, and low-producing plants.

The number of plants of the same variety needed to prevent this from happening depends on the array itself. For example, beans need around 20 plants, while corn needs a minimum of 200 plants to prevent genetic bottlenecking. I advise planting as many plants of the same variety as you can and saving some of those seeds. Then, every other year or so, introduce new genetic variation into your garden by buying the same variety of seeds (or swapping them) from a trusted source and adding a few of those into your garden so they can pollinate each other.

Not Storing Seeds Properly

This problem can include not following the proper steps or procedures beforehand or simply not ensuring the conditions for storage are favorable and consistent. But it can also include not keeping your seeds away from potential pests like rats or mites that can eat or contaminate them. That's why I always recommend glass jars for seed storage (especially if you live in an area where pests are a known issue)—they do a great job of keeping pests out of your seed stashes.

IN SUMMARY

You might only need some of the tools we mentioned in this chapter. Consider your gardening and seed-saving goals before you run out and buy things you don't need. From those goals, you can list tools you will use and need. For example, if you only plan on growing one variety of fruit and vegetables in your garden because you have limited space, you won't need blossom bags.

Seed saving and all the steps and considerations surrounding it can be time-consuming and overwhelming at first. But the steps are there for a reason. The main things to keep in mind are:

- allow the fruit to become overripe on the plant, just to be safe
- collect the seeds
- clean the seeds
- dry the seeds
- package and label the seeds
- store the seeds in proper conditions
- maintain a simple but efficient system of organization
- test the germination rates every year

- introduce new seeds every other year for genetic variation (not necessary for all crops)

Keeping your seeds organized and stored under the proper conditions is vital to retain their germination rates and vigor. In the next chapter, we'll go into more detail on exactly when and how you should harvest seeds so you can be sure you're saving only the best for the next season.

Now that the technicalities are out of the way and you have a better idea of setting up a system that will work for you, we're moving on to bigger things. And by more significant things, I mean big, juicy yields and how to harvest the best seeds!

4

HARVESTING SEEDS LIKE A PRO

Harvesting seeds sounds pretty simple. You pick the seeds; what more is there to do? Well, harvesting seeds is like a treasure hunt for a seed-saving enthusiast. And there's a lot more to it than you might think. Every plant is different, and their seeds are unique, with varied requirements for harvest to give them the best chance at reaching full maturity (and therefore withstanding storage) and resulting in a better next generation.

WHAT YOU'LL NEED

Depending on the crop type you plan on growing, you might only need some things listed here. But to avoid potential injuries (to you or the plant), here's a list of tools you'll need when harvesting seeds:

- Gloves: Protection from potential thorns and spikes to protect you from skin-irritating plants, insect bites, or being cut by leaves or stems.

- Eye protection: You can protect your eyes with items like clear goggles. The last thing you want is to have plant debris stuck in your eye for days, trust me.
- Scissors or pruners: Use these tools to cut stems and seed heads to avoid harming the plant by harshly pulling on it.
- Nutcrackers: If you're growing nuts or need to crack open hard shell coverings or husks, you'll need them.
- Trays, buckets, or bags: Essential for collecting your seed harvest and drying them out.

WHEN TO HARVEST

Timing is everything. One thing all plants have in common regarding harvesting seeds is that it's best to leave the fruit on the plant until it shows signs of being overripe. This stage will look different in each type of crop. For example, peppers shrivel, tomatoes go soft and squishy, and pea or bean pods dry out and turn brown.

A rule you can follow here is that if you need clarification on whether the fruit is ripe enough, leave it on the plant for a few more days. Also, fruit dropping off the plant by themselves indicates that the seeds have reached maturity and are ready to be collected, processed, and stored.

There's some nuance involved in harvesting seeds from different types of crops, such as annuals, biennials, perennials, and self-incompatible crops. Let's first discuss what these different classifications mean.

Annual Crops

Annuals (as you might already know) are plants that don't grow back after winter. Instead, they die off and must be re-sowed or replanted yearly. Self-fertile (or self-pollinating) crops are the easiest to save seeds from. This simplicity is especially true if you only have one type or variety of each plant because the likelihood of accidental cross-pollination (and, therefore, getting hybrid seeds) is rare in self-fertile plants.

This method is where you'll save the most money when it comes to gardening since saving your annual seeds will result in you not having to buy them yearly. As with all seed harvesting, you should allow the fruit and seed to ripen or become overripe on the plant. You can even wait for the plant to turn brown before retrieving the fruit and seeds, though this step isn't necessary.

Self-pollinating crops are known to be the easiest to grow in your home garden. A few examples of self-pollinating annuals you might want to grow in your garden and save seeds from include tomatoes, peppers, lettuce, eggplant, peas, and beans.

Biennial Crops

Biennials are crops that will stay alive for two years and typically won't flower or produce fruit or seeds in the first year. And even if they do show signs of flowering prematurely (within the first year), it's typically advised to pinch or cut these buds off so the plant's energy goes towards establishing the plant in the first year, which results in a much better yield in the second year.

The most apparent issue with biennials is you don't get a yield or any seeds to save for a whole year. That is why, if you want seeds every year from your biennials, you should plant a handful of them every year. This method means that, yes, in the first year, you'll have no seeds to save, but after that, you'll have a loop system where you have fruit and seeds every year. Let me explain:

- First year: You plant the first batch of seeds, and those seeds develop and become established for a whole year. There will be no seeds or produce to harvest this year.
- Second year: You plant another batch of seeds to develop over the next year. The first batch of biennials starts flowering and producing fruit. Once the fruit from the first batch of biennials is ready for harvesting, you can save some seeds. The first batch of biennials starts to die off over the next few months.
- Third year: You plant another batch of seeds to grow and develop over the next year. The second batch of seeds starts flowering and producing fruit and seeds, after which they will die off.
- Repeat this process, planting new seeds yearly and harvesting from last year's crops.

If this process sounds too complicated, or you need more space, save as many seeds as possible from a single harvest every other year. Some common examples of biennial crops are carrots, onions, beets, garlic, and parsley.

Perennial Crops

Perennials are plants with long life spans (more than two years) and do not fall under the classification of trees or shrubs. Perennials might go through a cycle where the plant is inactive in the off-season (usually during the winter), but they come back and produce flowers, fruit, and seeds every year in continuation.

You can aim for a garden with primarily perennial crops and a few annual crops. This strategy reduces the time and effort you need to propagate or sow seeds.

Examples of perennials include strawberries, blueberries, asparagus, chives, mint, and some spinach varieties.

Self-Incompatible Crops

A plant is self-incompatible when it can't be fertilized by itself, not even if it is hermaphroditic (it has both male and female parts on the same plant or flower). This classification means the plant can recognize when fertilized with its pollen and outright reject it. This distinction prevents inbreeding (a loss of genetic variety) and encourages environmental adaptation.

A self-incompatible plant will produce fruit (and therefore seeds) if exposed to pollen from a different plant (of the same variety). In layperson's terms, you need more than one of the same variety of plants to acquire a successful yield.

Most brassicas, such as cabbage, cauliflower, and broccoli, are self-incompatible along with certain other types of fruit, such as pineapples, cherries, citrus fruits, and apples.

HARVESTING FLOWER SEEDS

The key to a thriving garden is adding flowers that attract pollinators and predatory insects (which helps with pest control). You'll also want to save seeds from these plants (even if you only plant perennial flowers such as yarrow or coneflowers).

Harvesting seeds from flowers is a different process than harvesting seeds from fruit. However, it's not difficult at all. You can reap most flower seeds by allowing the flower to dry before clipping it off and shaking it upside down into a paper bag. The seeds should come loose and drop into the bag with minimal effort. If they don't, it usually means the flowers have yet to dry out enough.

Some flower seeds, such as sunflower and calendula seeds, need to be soaked in water for a few days before being dried again (for one to three weeks) for storage.

Seeds are plant embryos, so thinking of the seed-collecting process as collecting tiny gifts of nature is accurate. Many techniques make harvesting these pre-plant babies easy and time-efficient. Some seeds are more straightforward to harvest than others, but once you acquire the knowledge, you can collect seeds like a pro.

BASIC METHODS OF SEED COLLECTION

You'll likely get away with some basic approaches to harvesting seeds for most of your crops. In nature, seeds must fall when the time is ready without much struggle, so a future generation is unavoidable.

In general, seeds from annual crops are more straightforward to harvest than perennials. This statement is accurate because perennial seeds have the luxury of time for the husk or pod to break down before the seeds germinate (usually after being in the soil for several seasons or even years). Meanwhile, with annuals, the seeds need to be readily available so that when the fruit drops to the ground, it will grow a new plant by the following year.

This urgency is also why perennial seeds are more challenging to grow than annuals. Most perennial seeds need to go through specific conditions before they germinate—spending winters in frozen soil, being pecked at, or even being eaten and expelled by animals. These processes break down oils and wax coatings, softening hard shells that inhibit germination. This exposure ensures the seed germinates when the external conditions are just right.

The following basic seed collection techniques can work for both annual and perennial crops:

Hand-Picking

This one is self-explanatory. The process is manual, whether you're picking pods, heads, or the seed itself right from the plant. You already do this with your fruits and veggies if you have a home garden. It's the most basic and straightforward way to gather seeds.

Shaking or Beating

This technique can go hand-in-hand with hand-picking (no pun intended). When it comes to seed capsules and heads, the seed in them will require some form of dislodgement before you can dry and store them. Shaking or beating ripe seed heads over a tarp or large container is efficient. However, this method is best for crops where seeds simultaneously mature since you risk dislodging immature seeds with this method.

A few examples of common garden crops and flowers that hold their seeds in seed heads or capsules include dill, coriander, lettuce, most brassicas or mustard varieties, carrots, onions, cone-flowers, marigolds, and alliums.

Threshing

This technique separates seeds from other plant material like stalks, stems, leaves, husks, and even what's left over from seed heads and pods. The harvested plant material containing the seeds is dried before the threshing begins. You can carefully crush seed pods and heads to expose the seeds. You can thresh seeds attached to stems or surrounded by leaves by pulling the stalks through a fork or metal comb.

Threshing is less labor-intensive than shaking or beating individual seed heads, especially if you have a lot of seeds to separate. You can separate several common garden crops by threshing the seeds from plant material, including soybeans, lentils, chickpeas, and sunflowers.

Winnowing

Winnowing is typically the next step after threshing. Once you've released all the seeds from their pods, heads, and capsules or separated them from unusable plant material, the seeds are still typically mixed in with a decent amount of debris. Winnowing is the process of isolating the seeds from everything else. A simple way to do this is to take a handful of your debris and seed mixture, drop it from a few feet above a tarp or large container, and allow the wind to blow through it. The heavy seeds will fall straight down (back onto the tarp or into the large container) while the dry, light plant material will blow away.

To make this process more efficient, or if the wind is lacking, you can use an electrical fan to help things along. It would help if you did this work outside; otherwise, you'll be sweeping up dust and plant debris around the house for weeks.

HARVESTING DIFFICULT SEEDS

As mentioned, most seeds in your garden will be easy to harvest or collect, but some of them can be a real pain in the pod if you know what I mean. Some seeds are incredibly tiny, which makes them harder to harvest and clean (or debride) in preparation for storage.

You must carefully take some seeds out of hard shells or pods, which can lead to physical injuries (to both you and the seed). Some seed heads or pods explode when you break them open. Climbing plants or trees might make the fruit or seeds hard to reach.

Your safety is the most crucial factor when dealing with complex harvesting processes. Here is how to protect yourself from getting hurt when harvesting seeds:

Wear Protective Clothing

This suggestion includes wearing gardening gloves, long-sleeved pants and shirts, closed-toe shoes, masks, and protective glasses (especially when threshing, winnowing, or breaking open pods or shells). Many plant materials can irritate, cut, scratch, or even cause allergic reactions (or rashes) on your skin. Not to mention, there might be thorns or small insects that can bite or sting you.

Use the Proper Equipment

Continuously pulling on the plant to harvest fruit, vegetables, or seed pods and heads can damage the plant and lead to you being cut or hurt. Use pruners or scissors to cleanly and gently cut the stems to separate the fruit or seed heads from the plant. Always be careful when working with sharp tools to avoid cutting or nicking yourself. Also, remember to sterilize your tools between uses (and intermittently while using them) to protect the plants and yourself from getting or spreading potential infections or diseases.

QUALITY CONTROL

Seeds that are too old, were harvested too early, or are missing a live embryo on the inside will not germinate and grow. It's essential to take the necessary steps to ensure the seeds you save are healthy and viable. There are a few ways you can go about implementing quality control before and during the seed-storing process:

- Initial and ongoing germination tests: you need to perform annual germination tests to ensure optimal storage conditions. However, you should also do an initial germination test beforehand. This method is the most accurate way to determine the germination rate of your seeds. It would be best to take the sample (10 seeds minimum) from the same batch and make it a completely random selection.
- According to the water float test, any seed that floats in water after being harvested is considered a "dead" seed. Meaning it has no embryo inside and is not viable to save. However, while there might be some truth to this belief, it is certainly not trustworthy or accurate for all types of seeds. The water float test is only reliable for certain species of seeds within the legume and mint family.
- Physical inspection: Seeds that appear malformed, moldy, or have already started sprouting are not viable and will likely fail to germinate. It's worth mentioning that a variation in seed color doesn't necessarily indicate a dead or damaged seed, so don't discard those but instead investigate further and isolate them, just to be safe—seeds that are a different color than what's considered normal for a specific plant type might be indicative of a fungal, viral, bacterial, or genetic condition.

WHEN IT COMES TO PLANTING

The entire purpose of this book is to provide you with all the necessary knowledge and information you need to harvest and store your seeds effectively. However, some seeds need some "special treatment" before you sow them; otherwise, the germination rate of those seeds will be poor.

Most seeds enter a dormancy phase after they dry out, which enables us to store them for long periods (and a big reason why thoroughly drying your seeds is such a crucial step in the whole process). However, certain seeds have an inherited dormancy to ensure the seed only germinates when the conditions are just right. This phenomenon provides the plant's survival.

There are two main types of pre-sowing treatments: scarification and stratification. These pre-sowing treatments aim to overcome obstacles preventing some seeds from germinating. These obstacles usually include a state of endogenous dormancy (chemicals and genetic factors that affect the embryo itself, which generally requires cold stratification) or exogenous dormancy (a hard seed coating through which water can't penetrate, which requires scarification).

It's important to mention that scarifying or stratifying a seed must be done before you want to plant or sow the seeds. If you do this step before you store the seed, the seed will likely die during storage.

Scarification

Scarification is usually necessary for seeds that have a thick or waterproof seed coating. Water needs to be able to penetrate the outer layer of the seed before it can germinate. This condition is a form of exogenous dormancy—when conditions outside of the seed embryo prevent germination.

A simple test method is to soak a few in water for at least 24 hours and take a picture right before and after. If the seed doesn't absorb water (it doesn't appear to have increased in size after soaking), it will benefit from scarification.

There are a few ways you can go about scarifying a seed. The most common method is mechanical scarification, using a knife, file, or sandpaper to weaken or break the seed coating so water can penetrate and be absorbed more effectively. This method works best on large seeds, such as seeds from pumpkins, melons, and legumes, since trying to do this with smaller seeds can damage the seed, rendering it unable to germinate.

You can freeze smaller seeds for a few weeks before thawing them again. This step will weaken the seed coat enough or cause micro tears through which water can then penetrate better.

Stratification

Stratification has to do with the characteristics of the embryo itself, meaning that the embryo in the seed contains hormones or growth inhibitors that stay active until certain conditions are present. Sometimes, seeds that require stratification also have a hard seed coating.

Without going into too much of the science behind it, these hormones and growth inhibitors (and often accompanying hard seed coatings) aim to ensure a seed stays protected and doesn't germinate in the middle of winter because a seedling will never survive those conditions.

Summer crop seeds require heat stratification, meaning they germinate better when outdoor temperatures are warmer during summer's first few weeks. This type of stratification involves only sowing your seeds when the weather warms up (and remember to trap that heat using a greenhouse or transparent container).

To cold-stratify your seeds, pop them in the fridge or freezer. Remember that the time that seeds need to be stratified will depend on the species. Some plant seeds only need a week in the refrigerator, whereas others might require three months. It would help if you researched the specific seeds and variety to determine how long the seed needs stratification.

I can say that freezing and thawing seeds seem more effective for improving germination rates than keeping them at a constant fridge-like temperature. Stratifying seeds in the fridge raises the chances of mold growing on them (though the chance of mold in the refrigerator is still much less than in room temperature conditions). Check on your seeds regularly and ensure they're adequately dried.

An easier way to stratify your seeds is to sow them when the weather turns chilly enough and leave them be. This method works best with plants that are familiar with the local climate. However, doing it this way (even though it's less work) gives you less control over the process. It might lead to the seeds sprouting (and immediately dying from the cold) if you sow them too soon, and you also risk pests or rodents eating them.

Hand Pollination

There are a few reasons why you should consider manually pollinating your plants. The first is if your plants are in an area where pollinators can't quickly get to them (inside the house or if you live in an urban area). The second is if you have more than one variety of a particular plant that can cross-breed (for example, you grow chilies and bell peppers in the same gardening space).

Even self-fertile flowers have a chance of cross-pollinating, which can be an issue if you're planning on saving the seeds for next year's crops, if you want to donate them, or if you plan on swapping them out. When saving seeds, the motto is always "Better safe than sorry."

You don't need to hand-pollinate your crops if you're growing a single variety of all your crops. Still, if you have multiple crops in the same family that can cross-pollinate, you must isolate and hand-pollinate self-incompatible varieties. Or you'll at least have to separate, and hand pollinate a few flowers on each plant and save only the seeds from these specific fruits or flowers.

Hand pollination is the act of manually pollinating a flower. And it's easier than you imagine it to be. You only need a small, fluffy paintbrush, knowledge, and practice.

First, a little anatomy lesson: for a plant to be pollinated or fertilized, pollen from the stamen of a male flower needs to reach the pistil of a female flower. You'll need to look up what your specific crops' male and female plants look like so you know where to find the pollen and where to transfer it. Some species of plants can only be male (carrying pollen) or female (containing seeds), meaning you have to have both to get a yield.

The good news is that most crops are hermaphroditic, meaning every flower has both male and female reproductive parts, or every plant contains male and female flowers nearby. These are usually easy to hand pollinate since they require you to shake the entire plant so the pollen falls off the stamen and can float onto any nearby pistil. However, this isn't always the case, as some hermaphroditic flowers are also self-incompatible (like brassicas).

To hand pollinate female flowers, take your paintbrush and dab it on the stamen of a few male flowers before dabbing the loaded brush onto the center of a female flower.

You'll have to take pollen from a different plant for self-incompatible crops. Take broccoli, for instance, which is both a hermaphroditic and a self-incompatible crop (meaning it has male and female flowers but will reject pollen from the same plant). To hand-pollinate crops like broccoli, go around and load your brush with pollen from a different broccoli plant. An example of the strategy I find helpful and easy is as follows:

1. Collect only pollen from plant A.
2. Move to plant B and pollinate all the female flowers before collecting pollen from plant B.
3. Move to plant C and pollinate all the female flowers before collecting pollen from plant C.
4. When you get to the last plant, fertilize it with the previous plant's pollen before collecting pollen and going back to pollinate plant A.

Remember that you'll need to cover your flowers with blossom bags before the flowers even open to prevent cross-pollination. Only take the bag off the flower (or cluster of flowers) you're pollinating by hand and immediately put it back on afterward. Keep the bag on until the plant starts fruiting.

You must thoroughly clean the brush if you're using it on crops within the same family tree (when hand-pollinating broccoli right after you've done the cauliflower, for example). You can do this by wiping it on a clean cloth, but rinsing it under running water is the best option.

REMEMBER

It's important to sterilize your harvesting or gardening tools frequently, especially if you're using them on a plant that looks diseased, pest-ridden, or infected to prevent contaminating healthy plants. Also, to avoid future problems, don't save seeds from plants that look like they might have genetic diseases (or from plants that fail to thrive).

Harvesting seeds comes down to making sure the seeds mature, which is as easy as leaving the fruit or pod attached to the plant for as long as possible. Some seeds also require some extra steps during the harvesting process.

Sowing the Seeds of Knowledge to Save the Seeds of Life

"The best way to predict the future is to create it."

— PETER DRUCKER

Seed saving is an often overlooked area when it comes to gardening guides, but we only have to return to that shocking fact about lettuce varieties to see how important it is. From 500 types of lettuce to just 36 in 80 years! Unless we do something now, this is only going to continue.

As small-scale gardeners, it's hard to imagine that we'd have that much effect simply by saving seeds, but imagine the impact we could have if we all did it. All it takes is a mass commitment to preserving biodiversity, and we can make an incredible difference – and the sheer number of people moving toward sustainable gardening practices is enough to show that the motivation exists. Plus, the benefits to the individual gardener are immense – the money savings alone are enough to convince most people that saving their seeds is the way forward.

However, this is an area that is seldom targeted at gardeners who are new to the practice, and there's quite often an assumption that people know what to do. My goal with this book was to make the practice accessible to anyone, no matter how little they might know about seeds or saving and preserving them effectively. And now, just as a garden relies on its pollinators to spread its seeds, I'd like to ask you for your help in spreading this information – and the good news for you is that it will take you no more than a few minutes.

By leaving a review of this book on Amazon, you'll show new readers where they can find everything they need to know to make a success of seed saving – and you'll inspire them to try it too.

Reviews help readers find the guidance they're looking for, so it's a sure way to spread important information like this.

Thank you so much for your support. It makes a huge difference.

Scan the QR code below

5

SUSTAINABLE GARDENING THROUGH SEED SAVING

You might not start seed saving with sustainability in mind, but you could take the credit for it anyway. Sustainable gardening and seed saving are more closely connected than expected.

I understand the thought process behind the question, "If everyone doesn't participate and get with the program, how much of a difference am I going to make in the grand scheme of things?" This thought process is also known as environmental apathy. People acknowledge climate change and the need to do things differently. Still, they can't find the motivation to do anything because they're unsure their actions will have any impact, so why bother doing anything?

While it's true that a handful of people living sustainably aren't going to reverse climate change or have a significant impact, this narrative of "I'll do it when everyone else does" isn't exactly helping—two words: double standard.

A decent percentage of the global population has environmental apathy. Imagine if everyone holding onto this mindset went ahead and lived more sustainably anyway. Yes, one person isn't going to make a difference, but what about 10% of 8.1 billion? And that's being liberal—way more people than that think they can't make a difference.

To clarify, I'm not saying all this to make you feel bad for not living sustainably or for doing anything that leaves a carbon footprint. I'm also not saying your goal should be to make your carbon footprint zero. The aim is improvement, making better choices, starting small, and doing your best.

One way you can do that is by looking into permaculture gardening techniques and principles and seeing where it takes you. I want you to remember that we don't have to force the world to live sustainably—we need to convince them it's possible and inspire them.

PERMACULTURE PRINCIPLES

The entire message and cause behind permaculture principles is about caring—not only about all other life forms on this earth but also about our impact on the future and what we leave behind. The only way to ensure the planet takes care of us for generations is for us to take care of it right now. We do that by living a sustainable lifestyle based on the 12 principles of permaculture, which are as follows:

Observe and Interact

Know your planting space inside and out. Know which areas get the most sun, shade, wind, and rain. You'll save so much time and effort if you're not trying to keep plants alive when they're growing in places where they have no business growing in the first place.

Catch and Store Energy

Store and use abundance by catching or redirecting rainwater, pickling or preserving fruits and vegetables so you can enjoy them during winter and even beyond, or investing in a solar system. There are so many ways to utilize naturally occurring energy creatively—all you need to do is think outside the box.

Obtain a Yield

The gardening goal is fresh produce, which means obtaining a good yield. Good planning from the start (and permaculture techniques) will pay off by reducing the maintenance needed in your garden and maximizing your yield's quality and size.

Apply Self-Regulation and Accept Feedback

When something isn't working, your garden will let you know. Your job is to observe and listen to what your garden tells you so you can get to and solve the problem's root cause. Let nature deal with nature; don't try to fight it because you will lose.

Use Renewable Resources and Services

Caring about the future means using resources that replenish themselves. This method ranges from planting perennial crops to composting to building your house so the sun's heat warms it up instead of relying on non-renewable energy sources.

Produce No Waste

Create closed-loop systems wherever you can. Only throw something away if it can't be repaired or reused in some other way. Examples of this strategy are feeding kitchen scraps to worms, using dried grass clippings or weeds for mulch, or repurposing plastic jars for propagating seeds or housing seedlings. Instead of throwing out a broken wooden chair, you can repair it, build an insect house, or make a side table or footstool. And if you can't avoid garnering plastic, use it for as long as possible. I've seen videos online of people making an outdoor area rug with single-use plastic bags. There's always a way!

Design From Patterns to Details

Only plant what your family enjoys eating to reduce waste. Plant your garden in zones based on what makes the most sense (herbs near the kitchen, hardy plants that need little attention further away, crops that prefer shade right next to a building). Map out routes around your garden and use every inch of space as nature would.

Integrate, Don't Segregate

This rule applies not only to your plants but also to your community. Share seeds, abundant produce, and tools amongst your neighbors to build community and encourage self-sufficiency.

Small, Slow Solutions

Permaculture has taught me that you can substitute everything or make yourself from scrap or affordable materials. Don't run to buy expensive or gimmicky tools if you're getting by just fine with what you have now (or if you can substitute or make it yourself).

Value Diversity

By now, you know how important diversity is in your garden. It comes down to placing only some of your eggs in one basket. You will have a more extensive variety of nutrient-dense food, and a diverse garden will be more resilient to pests.

Use Edges and Margins

Maximizing space means using all space you have: balconies, the edges of footpaths or driveways, or that corner of the yard where junk had accumulated for years. Get creative with it.

Respond to Change Creatively

One thing that's for sure in life is change, which can't be more true regarding gardening. The state of your garden can change overnight, even if you pull out all the stops to protect it from pests, wind, rain, hail, snow, and heat waves, so while you should come up with creative reasons to protect your garden, that also includes coming up with creative ways to solve problems.

Living a lifestyle as close to permaculture practices as possible seems extreme, and it can be. Living off the grid is only possible and plausible for some. Remember, even small changes are significant in the grand scheme of things. No matter how small of a step you take with it, it's still a step in the right direction and a good deed for the planet and our future.

THE CONNECTION

We previously discussed how seed saving benefits you and the environment: it makes you more self-reliant, preserves biodiversity and genetic material, saves money, and contributes to food security. And regardless of why you started gardening or saving seeds in the first place, much like a domino effect, it cultivates a sustainability mindset.

Think about it. More than likely, you went into starting a small garden in your backyard with little to no knowledge or experience. You wanted to know more as you've improved at keeping your garden alive. What's the best way to do this? What's the easiest way to do that? How can I keep this from happening again? How can I improve my yield and quality of produce?

You want all the information and to know what to do when challenges inevitably arise. But more than that, you've come to care about your garden and every plant in it. Your gardening journey has led to you appreciating nature more (like it did for me), so you want to do whatever you can to keep your garden alive, happy, and thriving.

Every tiny thing you do has the potential to create massive ripples and carry them to the person next to you. You contribute to more significance and change as you learn and share that knowledge with others.

Seed saving is connected to sustainability because it convinces you that you can make a difference in your life and future generations. It builds your confidence and leads you to conclude that it's easier than you thought. And with every step you take, your mind expands. You become comfortable learning and practicing new skills and ideas and gaining experience through trial and error.

It starts with planting a seed and ends with you doing everything possible to make better choices.

Your Carbon Footprint

Additionally, practicing seed saving reduces your carbon footprint by contributing to growing crops compatible with the local climate. Crops comfortable with the environment need less synthetic input from chemical fertilizers or pesticides.

Not buying seeds or seedlings from a store every year means less emissions and waste. Large-scale seed harvesting, drying, and packaging are possible with machines that produce harmful emissions and by-products. These machines also require maintenance, fuel, humans, etc. Distributing the seeds also involves long-distance transportation. Not only does this make the prices of seeds skyrocket, but it also poisons the environment.

Moreover, seed packaging material (often than not) contains plastic, packaging in flimsy plastic trays that typically break or rip when you're trying to get them out for transplanting (meaning you can't reuse them and end up needing to throw them away). By cutting out the middle man and saving your seeds, you save money and reduce your impact on the planet.

The Environment

Seed saving has a net positive influence on the environment. As mentioned earlier, it promotes biodiversity and resilience, which is incredibly important for us by strengthening our food security and for the future of gardening.

With every generation, your crops emerge stronger, meaning you are less likely to need to use chemical fertilizers and pesticides, and in doing so, you also preserve the health and quality of your soil. You also don't accidentally poison pollinators and predatory insects that visit your garden with nothing but good intentions and a positive impact.

An abundance of local plant foliage also attracts biodiversity in the form of insects and wildlife, which contributes massively to the overall health of your garden (and can act as a natural pest deterrent) and the local environment. A bustling garden is a happy garden.

SUSTAINABLE SEED SOURCES

There might come a time when you want to expand your garden, try a different variety of a specific crop, or build on your seed bank. Of course, getting seeds harvested locally is the best option, but if you need help finding someone to swap seeds with or there's a scarcity of local seed-saving communities in your area, you can still source seeds sustainably.

Source your seeds from reputable, certified organic, non-GMO seed suppliers. Additionally, you can find out if these companies have taken the Safe Seed Pledge or refer to trusted online growing guides for recommendations on the best varieties of crops for your climate or region.

Look up regional seed suppliers. It's better to buy seeds harvested a few towns over than from the store that could've gotten them from the other side of the world. Here's a short list of recommended companies to source your seeds from that all undertake organic and sustainable principles:

- Seed Savers Exchange
- High Mowing Organic Seeds

- Johnny's Selected Seeds
- Peaceful Valley/Grow Organic

SEED SAVING FOR YOU

While we're on sustainability, I want to mention one crucial consideration: your current gardening routine or schedule. If saving your seeds will interfere with your lifestyle, it won't be sustainable because you're likely going to stop doing it.

You need to seamlessly integrate seed saving into your current gardening routine for it to be worth doing. To do this work, you'll need to consider when to harvest the seeds for every crop and when you'll have some extra time to process, preserve, and store all the seeds.

That's why I recommend starting with only a few crops with seeds that are easy to harvest and require little additional effort. For example, if you're already setting aside an entire day for cutting up harvested fruits and vegetables every other week (to preserve, pickle, or freeze), you might rinse the seeds and put them aside to dry. If you're harvesting on a more regular basis, such as every day (so you have fresh produce for dinner), put the seeds aside and return to them when you have a few minutes (maybe while the sauce is simmering) so you can rinse them off and let them dry.

Keep in mind this suggestion is only an example. The best way to stick to something new is to adapt it to your current routine and lifestyle (not the other way around), or at the very least, make small and gradual changes so the process is manageable and sustainable.

By following this strategy, you make seed-saving work and don't need to dip into your minimal free time to keep up with it. Of course, you might have to rearrange your approach if you have a more extensive garden or save many seeds. Please find a way to make it work within your lifestyle and schedule, and play around with routines and time-saving tips until you find the most efficient method.

LEGAL CONSIDERATIONS

A patent grants individuals or organizations property rights to materials, processes, machinery, or improvements to any of the formerly mentioned. This distinction means that companies or individuals can legally prevent (and pursue) anyone who isn't them from making, using, selling, or distributing the product or manufacturing processes that they invented or created.

So, not just seeds that can be patented but also the processing method. There are some restrictions on what can and can't be patented. The methods or materials must be unique or nonobvious, recognizable, and described in clear and definite terms.

Legally, you can't save seeds from patented crop varieties without explicit, documented permission from the patent holder. Nor can you sell or distribute these seeds. Even collecting seeds from plants on public land requires a permit.

To ensure you do everything by the book and prevent potential legal troubles, always verify that an individual or business entity has yet to claim the seeds you buy, receive, and swap. You can do this in a few ways:

Check the Labels or Packaging

Seeds you buy from the store will disclose patent information regarding the specific seed variety. There will usually be something on the packaging like: "Patent [number]" or "Pat. [number]." If you're looking to plant crops you can save the seeds from, avoid seeds with this information on the packaging.

Talk to Your Distributor

If you're swapping seeds or getting them from anyone who functions independently, ask where their "seed dealer" got them. However, don't just take their word for it. If you plant these seeds, before you harvest and save the seeds, make sure you identify the variety and do some research.

Ask the Internet

You can look up active or pending patents on websites like Patent Public Search, Global Dossier, Patent Application Information Retrieval (PAIR), or look up Patent and Trademark Resource Centres (PTRCs).

Shifting towards a more sustainable and eco-friendly way of living will not happen overnight. There are also a lot of mental obstacles you need to overcome, such as environmental apathy. The mere fact that you're considering saving seeds is a monumental leap in the right direction.

Refrain from overwhelming yourself with the burden of trying to do everything right or always making the right decisions. Start by mastering seed saving, then revisit this topic later; know that you're already coming ahead by saving seeds from your garden.

6

PEST AND DISEASE MANAGEMENT IN SEED SAVING

A happy and healthy garden starts with the seeds you choose to grow. You can prevent future genetic conditions or diseases by ensuring that the seeds aren't affected by them during the growing, harvesting, and preservation process.

PEST AND DISEASE IMPACT ON SEED QUALITY

Seeds growing mold or fungi in storage will significantly affect and, in most cases, destroy the viability of the seed for apparent reasons. But did you know that the plant's health can also affect the quality and resilience of the resulting seed? This outcome occurs because pests and other ailments caused by bacteria or fungi lower the protein content in seeds—and protein is like a building block of life.

It's simple: an unhealthy plant, caused by a genetic defect or external disease, is most likely to produce an ill seed, and a less-than-optimal seed won't grow into a productive plant. If you save seeds from sick plants or try to grow unhealthy seeds, you will start a cycle where every generation becomes weaker and more vulnerable. That reasoning is why you should only save seeds from your best and healthiest crops and get rid of any plants or seeds that look suspicious.

Moreover, a contaminated seed can infect other seeds around them. So, if you store a "bad" seed with other "good" seeds, you risk losing the entire batch. However, this outcome only occurs with external pathogens (like mold, fungi, bacteria, etc.) and not genetic diseases.

Certain fungi that grow on plants and seeds (most commonly grains and nuts) produce what's known as mycotoxins and can lead to adverse health effects like immune deficiency, kidney damage, and even cancer when ingested. Mycotoxins are heat resistant (unless you're heating your food to 500°F, they're still there) and can take years to break down entirely.

Beneficial fungi (mycorrhiza) grow alongside your plant's roots and enhance the plant's nutrient and water intake. Still, it will never rise above ground or negatively affect your plant. So, as a general rule of thumb, if there's any sign of fungi or mold growing on your plants, produce, or seeds, dispose of them immediately (do not compost or mulch with moldy grain and nuts since you run the risk of introducing mycotoxins into the soil and the rest of your garden).

You've probably seen what mold looks like on food (such as fruits and vegetables), but spotting a fungal infection on seeds can be trickier because they're much smaller. Signs of fungi are discoloration and a shriveled or "hairy" appearance.

Pests and Seedborne Diseases

Seedlings are susceptible to many pests, like beetles, worms, slugs, and snails. However, your seeds aren't safe from pests either and are typically the target of insects (like mites, ants, moths, and crickets), rodents, and birds. The important thing is getting to the seed before they do, and proper storage containers will prevent rodents and other pests from getting into the free buffet that is your seed bank.

Seedborne diseases, on the other hand, happen when a seed succumbs to a pathogen (fungi, virus, or bacteria), which carries over to the next generation of plants due to the seed's exposure.

You can prevent pathogens from infecting your seeds by maintaining proper garden hygiene. Keeping your plants healthy and pest-free is the first step to having and saving healthy seeds. To do so, follow basic gardening precautions like:

- You are choosing healthy seeds and plants to start your garden before even getting into seed saving.
- Grow patent-free, disease-resistant, locally adapted (or hcirloom) plant varieties.
- Harvesting at the proper time to ensure the seeds are mature.
- Practicing crop rotation yearly and ensuring soil health and quality are up to par.
- Inspect your garden regularly for diseased plants, pest infestations, and weeds, and implement ways to reduce or prevent these issues naturally.
- Keep gardening tools clean and disinfect them between uses.
- You are introducing diversity into your garden concerning plant species and beneficial insects.

- You are only harvesting seeds from healthy plants. Additionally, you can isolate plants you plan on saving seeds from by growing them in pots where you have more control over their exposure.

Since moths, ants, and other garden pests like to feast on seeds, you should be looking for any indication that your fruits or flowers are being eaten alive. Holes in the fruit or hollowed-out seeds can be hard to spot, so inspect the seeds thoroughly.

Timing is another crucial element in harvesting seeds. As previously mentioned, you want to leave the fruit or flowers that carry the seeds attached to the plant for as long as possible. However, if your garden has a pest problem, harvest the fruit or flowers when they're ripe enough. You can add a note on the batch of seeds stating that harvesting was earlier than you would've liked or that pests were present.

Given enough time, anything is possible. If you know rodents or specific pest problems exist in your area, take extra precautions to protect your seeds in storage. Please familiarize yourself with common plant diseases and how to prevent or treat them (and don't save seeds from sick plants). This reasoning is also why you should save more seeds than you think you'll need—if one batch turns out to be infertile (for whatever reason), infected, or mutated, you have more.

Take care of your garden to prevent the common problems, and you'll figure out the rest with patience and experience.

7

COMMUNITY AND SEED SHARING

We had to barter before we used pieces of paper with numbers printed for payment. Even though gold and silver existed, people often traded goods and services with each other because they knew that sharing resources amongst the community was important. Many people didn't have much back then, but they had their skills and a generous, caring community.

If you've ever been part of a close-knit community, you'll know what I'm talking about. Sharing is the whole point. When you share knowledge, skills, and experience, you contribute to and invest in the future. When you share kindness, you're contributing to the strength of the community.

There's a reason why many people feel so fulfilled when they give back to others in the form of charity or kindness. As cliché as it might sound, when you share seeds, you share life.

WHY COMMUNITY IS IMPORTANT

The 2020 pandemic brought the whole world to a screeching, crashing halt. The first few weeks in quarantine were manageable; people were in denial, and the excitement of working from home (for those who could) made everything seem less scary. Of course, the number of lives lost during that time is and was horrific.

Nevertheless, people were coping with the uncertainty and dread. Sleeping in for an extra hour helped with the added stress and uncertainty. But as days of isolation turned into weeks of zero contact with friends and family, people started going a little stir-crazy. Introverts naturally managed to last a bit longer than the average person, but even they got to a point where the lack of socialization became mental torture.

We tried filling the void. Many people picked up old hobbies, started learning new skills, or worked on self-improvement (primarily by prioritizing their physical and mental health). The economic uncertainty that the pandemic brought on incentivized a decent portion of the population to start their home gardens (which was a big reason for the seed shortage during that time). All of that is fantastic!

But the thing is, communication and community are not desires—they're needs. It's a basic human need. It provides us with a sense of belonging and more significant purpose, serves as a source of connectedness and unity, and fosters understanding, support, and growth by exposing us to people who share similar or even alternative points of view.

Being part of a community broadens our horizons by giving us access to knowledge, experience, generosity, encouragement, and a more profound sense of fulfillment. It's there—all you need to do is reach for it.

START BY SHARING

You can join a seed-saving or gardening community before you've saved enough seeds. Join local social media groups or pages and watch for gatherings. Put yourself out there by attending farmer's markets and conversing with the other shoppers or the sellers.

However, once you have some extra seeds to share, why not? Think of it as an act of good faith. There are many simple yet practical ways to share seeds:

- Invite local gardeners to exchange seeds.
- Donate your seeds to local schools, community gardens, or seed libraries.
- Make cards (greeting cards, birthday cards, or other occasion cards) from recycled paper and embed seeds into them (this way, you can tear the card into pieces and plant them directly in the ground).
- Make DIY packets with seeds and some easy-to-follow instructions for beginner-friendly seeds and gift them to kids, friends, or family members to kickstart their gardening journey.

You establish rapport with community members by spreading and sharing the seeds (and love). You'll find that gardening communities are typically friendly, warm, and inviting.

Organizing a Seed Swap

Hosting a seed-swapping event is optional. You're welcome to attend existing events and get all your seed-swapping needs met that way. But if you are more daring and ambitious and have what it takes, hosting your seed swap can be a great way to make a name for yourself within your gardening community (or even beyond).

Whether you want to keep it small or make it elaborate, there are a few things to keep in mind beforehand:

Who's Your Audience?

Consider how many people there will be, how many seeds they might bring, and their experience. However, it's impossible to have a way to know this information with certainty in advance; it will largely depend on how and where you promote the event.

How Will They Know?

For people to know there's a seed swap happening, you need to spread the word. You can do this by making a couple of flyers and putting them up on notice boards at local garden centers, health-food stores, community bulletin boards, or local social media networking pages. If you have some friends who are into gardening, you can invite them to a small get-together and swap seeds amongst each other only.

Where Will You Host It?

You might need to acquire a venue depending on how many people will attend your seed swap event. You can partner with local gardening groups, schools, libraries, or community centers to find a suitable indoor or outdoor venue for free (or at a way more affordable price).

Do You Need Sponsors or Donors?

You can reach out to local nurseries, gardening clubs, restaurants, caterers, or seed banks to donate towards or sponsor the event (again, depending on how big the event will be). Businesses will be more likely to sponsor events or donate if there are a lot of opportunities for publicity or marketable audiences. If the event is small, you likely won't need sponsors or donations, but it certainly can't hurt to ask. If you don't ask, the answer is always "no."

Will You Need Volunteers?

Even at a small seed-swapping event, you'll need help with setup, clean-up, etc. You can approach friends and family members for help or go to outside sources like social media platforms or post flyers. Make sure there's some incentive for the volunteers.

How Will You Set Up the Venue?

Offer refreshments in the form of beverages and snacks. Sprinkle in a few educational displays between the seed exchange tables. Include demonstrations, talks, games ("identify the seed," for example), or raffles to keep people engaged and entertained.

What Will the Cost Be?

Decide whether the event will be free or people must pay a small fee. If you are charging people, the aim should be to cover the costs, not to make a profit. Remember, you want to join or bring the community together, so it should be a fun day that encourages everyone to participate and leave with a willingness to attend again.

Share Your Knowledge

Spreading information and education is no one's responsibility, but we wouldn't be where we are today if people didn't take on this vital task. You don't need to go out of your way to educate others or convert people to the seed-saving lifestyle, but taking on that responsibility does benefit us all and ensures the future of the plant species and seed-saving tradition. But don't be a nuisance, either. People who are interested and eager to know more already have one foot in the door.

You may not have all the knowledge and information yet, but you can collaborate with people who know more and share what you have learned (even if it's just a heart-warming story about your journey and experiences).

By organizing workshops, giving presentations at schools, volunteering at local seed banks or community gardens, and being hands-on wherever you can, you contribute to keeping this vital tradition alive!

SEED SWAPPING ONLINE

The internet can be a horrible place, but it has also made connecting with a larger community more accessible. Yes, being able to come together and physically swap seeds with the locals is excellent, but the internet is a close second if you don't have the option or opportunity.

Going online to swap seeds with strangers has its downsides. For example, you can never trust whether the person on the other end is who they say they are or will do what they say. And it would be best if you were always cautious about keeping your personal information private. But it makes getting a hold of specific varieties you want to grow in your garden easier.

You can share or trade seeds online through trustworthy online platforms:

- Seed Savers Exchange
- Southern Exposure Seed Exchange
- Dave's Garden
- GardenWeb's forums
- BASIL

You can also check out social media platforms for seed-saving groups:

- Great American Seed Swap (Facebook)
- "r/seedswap" (Reddit)
- Other blogs, forums, or websites that allow their members to make requests and offers for seeds

CREATING YOUR OWN SEED BANK

It would help if you started your seed bank for many reasons, regardless of your goals. You might have a smaller stash if you're planning on simply storing seeds for personal use, but you can also take it further if you have the means and want to share your seeds with the community.

What Is a Seed Bank?

Think of a seed bank as a personal insurance policy for your garden. You'll be able to plant the seeds and varieties you want to grow every year for free, and you're also sure of your future garden's production quality and vigor.

The proper definition of a seed bank is a facility (or designated space) for storing various types and varieties of seeds in a controlled environment. The purpose of a seed bank is to preserve genetic variation and to safeguard the supply and availability of all plant species.

Starting Small

Start a small-scale seed bank if you have limited space for storing the seeds or when you have a small garden. The key is to be creative: use envelopes or Ziploc bags instead of containers so that everything fits into a small cooler or insulated lunch bag.

If you have a small garden, you'll have a limited amount and variety of seeds. To grow your collection, consider swapping seeds with your local gardening community. By doing so, you can expand your seed collection quickly.

The point is that you have to start somewhere. Don't be discouraged because you only have 50 tomato seeds in your seed bank. Don't feel like you're not a legitimate seed saver because you're using an old shoebox for your seeds. Your collection will grow quicker than you think with some perseverance and determination.

Always ensure you're employing and implementing the proper methods for harvesting, cleaning, drying, and storing your seeds. And make sure that, if you are swapping seeds, the person you're exchanging with is also following the correct practices.

Going Big

Get involved with other seed savers in your community by joining local farming groups and contacting commercially or privately owned seed banks. Many seed banks offer memberships that are free or require a small donation.

Furthermore, you can volunteer in community gardening programs, attend seed swap events, or start a community or local seed bank if there isn't one already (and if you have the means to do so). Creating a large-scale seed bank is no easy feat and will require you to:

- Acquire a seed inventory through local donations, exchanges, swapping seeds, or purchasing them yourself.
- Find a facility with the proper storage requirements if you outgrow your home.
- Establish rules for memberships.
- Recruit a team to manage daily operations such as inventory management, quality control, maintaining proper storage principles, etc. However, this requirement only applies once the business grows to a degree where it needs ongoing daily support and you need help to keep up with everything.
- Abide by any applicable bylaws or legal requirements.

Starting a business in the seed industry might not be your goal, and that's okay, too. You can also keep it small by creating a Facebook page, getting as many gardening and seed-saving enthusiasts to join, and then holding monthly get-togethers or seed-swapping events. However, you may also be completely content joining an existing seed-saving community group in your area.

Being a part of (or creating) a community that shares similar goals and interests is one of the most fulfilling things you can do in life. Even if you're not social, I guarantee you will enjoy joining a like-minded community and building your seed bank simultaneously.

Starting your seed bank (even on a small scale) with the idea of swapping, donating, or exchanging them means implementing strict storage and organizational practices to ensure seed viability, health, and seeds are true to type (or open-pollinated).

There's much to consider regarding seed saving and your ultimate goal, so start with one thing at a time. Perfect the steps before you go off script.

You don't have to jump into the deep end with seed saving. Organizing your seed-swapping event or starting your seed bank might sound exciting, but it's not a requirement. You can attend a few events and get involved before you make that leap. Make a few connections in the community first and see where it takes you (and consider whether this is what you want).

8

SEED PRESERVATION FOR COMMON GARDEN CROPS

Now that we've covered the basics, we will put all that knowledge into practice. This final chapter is a step-by-step guide for harvesting and preserving the most common beginner-friendly garden crops (fruits, vegetables, herbs, and flowers). Some of these crops are already in your garden.

What better way to hone and perfect your seed-saving skills than to use what we've learned throughout this book in your backyard? Remember: Before you'll be good at it, you'll be bad at it—getting good is the journey.

FRUIT

Arguably, the easiest plants to save seeds from are fruits. Typically, the seeds are in the fruit itself. All you need to do is separate it; that process is always straightforward. There are exceptions to the rule, like how bananas have transformed so much that there's barely any trace of seeds left where they were supposed to be. But bananas are hardly a beginner-friendly crop, so that's beside the point.

Tomatoes

"Knowledge is knowing that a tomato is a fruit. Wisdom is knowing not to put it in a fruit salad"(O'Driscoll, 2015). That quote always cracks me up. Tomatoes are easily the most common garden crop. They're a staple in gardens of all sizes, and for good reason. My dog once stole a tomato from the kitchen, and a couple of months later, a tomato plant was growing in the chicken pen. The point is tomatoes are easy to grow and maintain, delicious, versatile, and easy to save seeds from. Here's how to harvest tomato seeds:

1. Please wait until the end of the season before saving seeds from tomatoes to ensure they're ripe and ready. Start by picking an open-pollinated tomato right before you want to process and harvest the seeds.
2. Cut open the tomato and squeeze the seeds out (or scoop them out with a spoon) onto a plate or other broad, shallow container (or a glass jar if you're fermenting). You can use the remnants of the seedless tomato like any other tomato, but making purees or sauces with them works best.
3. You have a few options: you can spread everything out and let the seeds and pulp dry down for two to three weeks before picking out the seeds, rinsing, drying them again, and storing them; you can rinse the pulp away using a strainer or sieve before drying and storing them; or you can ferment the seeds and pulp (in a glass jar with water) for five days. Fermenting the seeds results in a better quality seed and a higher germination rate. If you plan to

save the seeds for a long time (longer than a couple of years), use the fermentation method.

4. Please make sure the seeds are dry before storing them. Do the fingernail test to check (if the seed leaves an imprint or feels like it has some give, let it dry for a couple more days). Avoid direct or even bright indirect sunlight during the drying time.

If dried and stored correctly, tomato seeds can be viable for up to twelve years.

Strawberries

Not only are strawberries the only fruit that carries seeds on the outside, but they also have a juicy secret—strawberries are not berries at all! They're known as "false fruits" and contain numerous tiny fruits. Essentially, each seed is a separate fruit attached to a receptacle (everything surrounding the individual fruits, including what they're bound to in the middle).

I'm not here to slander strawberries. We should all forgive them for their deceit. After all, who doesn't like fresh strawberries and wouldn't want strawberry plants in their garden? They're the perfect beginner crop you can plant anywhere you have an open spot of soil (as a ground-cover crop to keep the weeds at bay). But be warned, they spread very quickly if you don't keep an eye on those runners!

To harvest seeds from strawberries, here's what you're going to do:

1. Leave the fruit on the bush for as long as possible. At this point, it's standard procedure. Choose the biggest, boldest fruit from the healthiest plants to harvest your strawberries from.

2. Again, you have a few options to choose from when separating the seed from the fruit: use a toothpick to meticulously dislodge every individual seed from the strawberry into a plate or container (the most labor-intensive approach); cut thin slices of skin (with the seeds still intact) off the strawberry and place them on a paper towel to dry out for a week, and once they're dry you can rub the seeds off onto a plate relatively easy and dry them some more before storing them; or press the fruit through a fine mesh or strainer—the seeds will remain, and you can proceed with rinsing and drying them.

3. Whatever method you choose, it's always a good idea to rinse your seeds before drying them to eliminate any pulp or residue that might result in mold or fungi growth.

4. Most strawberry varieties need to be cold stratified, meaning they need a simulated winter to break them out of "dormancy" and increase their germination rate. To do this, place your seeds in the fridge for at least a month (let them come to room temperature by taking them out of the refrigerator for 24 hours) before planting them.

I want to note that strawberry seeds might very well germinate without a cold stratification process, but they will take much longer to do so, and your germination rate will be much lower.

Strawberry seeds can be stored for two to three years or even longer when frozen (though the germination rate will naturally decline with time).

Blueberries

Famously known for containing the highest levels of antioxidants than any other fruit or vegetable, blueberries are praised and labeled as a superfood and relatively easy to grow. But one thing about these powerfully healthy berries is that their seeds are so tiny that straining them through even the finest sieve will leave you empty-handed. However, where there's a will, there's a way. Here's what you do:

1. Harvest blueberries from multiple healthy plants.
2. Macerate the blueberries by blending them in a food processor or mashing them in a bowl with water.
3. Give your blueberry puree a good mix. The pulp will float to the top, and the seeds will sink to the bottom. Scoop off the floating pulp. You might have to add water, remix everything, and skim off the pulp until all is gone.
4. Pour off as much water as you can and scoop the seeds onto a paper towel. Dry them and store them like you would any other seed.
5. Blueberry seeds benefit from scarification (nicking the seed coating), but because the seeds are so tiny, you risk damaging them if you try to do this (even rubbing them on sandpaper might cut too deep). So, a more accessible and safer way to do this is to place the seeds on a damp paper towel in a Ziploc bag and place the bag in the freezer for at least 90 days. Then, defrost them and allow them to come to room temperature before you plan on sowing them. Freezing the seed will soften the coat enough to let the embryo break through it more easily.

Remember that blueberries are not self-fertile, so you must ensure you have enough genetic variation by having five or more of the same variety but with different parent plants (and introducing genetic variation every other year or so).

You can effectively store blueberry seeds for two years.

Cucumbers

Like tomatoes, botanists consider cucumbers a fruit because they grow from a flower and have seeds on the inside. But regardless of how you use them in your dishes (or skincare routine), they are easy to grow from seeds. However, harvesting seeds from cucumbers requires a delicate hand because the seeds are soft and have that gel seed capsule, just like tomato seeds.

The process of harvesting cucumber seeds is very similar to harvesting tomato seeds:

1. Cut your ripe, freshly harvested, healthy cucumber in half and scrape out the middle parts (with the pulp) into a glass jar with some water. Allow it to ferment for three to five days, and remember to stir daily.
2. Scoop or pour off everything that floated to the top after three to five days of fermentation.
3. Remove the seeds left at the bottom of the jar and rinse them before spreading them out on a tray lined with parchment paper or paper towels.
4. Leave the seeds to dry completely before labeling and storing them.

You can store cucumber seeds for up to five years.

Capsicums

Regarding capsicums, you will likely have chilies or bell peppers (or both) in your garden. Capsicums are easy to grow and versatile, making them a popular and common crop for any kitchen garden. As it turns out, saving the seeds from these beauties is also very straightforward:

1. Leave a few fruits on the plants until they wrinkle. This process can take months. Mark these fruits with a ribbon so you don't accidentally harvest them.
2. When you harvest the peppers or chilies, the seeds will fully mature and dislodge with minimal effort. Cut the fruit open and firmly shake or tap it over a plate or tray until no more seeds are inside. You can use the fruit in conserves, sauces, or stews as usual, although the texture might differ slightly.
3. Inspect the seeds and discard any that appear damaged, discolored (seeds are typically off-white), or smaller than the rest.
4. Rinse the seeds with a strainer or sieve, spread them out on a tray lined with paper towels or parchment paper, and let dry away from direct sunlight for at least a week. If you have a fine mesh screen, you can use it to dry the seeds (this way, you don't have to turn them every other day to ensure proper airflow). Do the fingernail test to check if they're dry enough; if unsure, let them dry for a couple more days and check again.

Capsicum seeds can remain viable for an astonishing 25 years when stored properly. However, a more realistic time frame (and for best germination rates) is under five years.

Pumpkin or Squash

Another multi-purpose, beginner-friendly crop to grow is pumpkins (or their little cousins: squash). These vibrant fruits are a must-have, from soups to veggie bakes to Halloween decorations.

The best thing about saving seeds from pumpkins or squash is that you can also eat them. The seeds contain manganese, vitamin K, and many other nutrients. Here's how you can save pumpkin seeds:

1. Cut open your overripe pumpkin and scoop out the seeds and pulp. Just like with the tomato and cucumber seeds, if you plan to store them for longer than a couple of years, opt for fermenting the seeds for five days. Otherwise, rinse everything and manually pick out the seeds from the pulp. Whether or not you ferment the seeds, spread them out on a tray with paper towels, parchment paper, or a mesh screen.
2. Dry the seeds in a dark, well-ventilated room for about two weeks or until they pass the fingernail test. Make sure you stir or turn the seeds every couple of days to make sure they dry evenly (unless you're using a mesh screen).
3. Once all the seeds are dry, pick out the most significant seeds to save for planting. More giant pumpkin seeds have a better chance of germinating. You can keep smaller seeds for eating; alternatively, you can blend them into a powder and add them back into your garden bed.

You can store pumpkin seeds for up to five years.

VEGETABLES

Unlike fruits, vegetables don't carry their seeds on the inside but rather in a pod, capsule, or flower. Despite that distinction, harvesting seeds from vegetables is far from rocket science. I will walk you through saving seeds from the most common garden vegetable crops in a few easy steps.

Brassicas

This category includes leafy greens like spinach, lettuce, kale, cabbage, Swiss chard, Brussels sprouts, cauliflower, and broccoli. The entire Brassica family tree grows similarly, so the methods for harvesting the seeds from various crops are identical.

The way collard or leafy greens make seeds is by sending out a long stalk (usually from the center of the plant but can be on the side depending on the type of brassica you're growing) from where the flower, and eventually the seed pods, will grow from. This process is called bolting and is relatively easy to identify: look for a stalk instead of a leaf! And it usually happens closer to the end of the season. To save brassica seeds, follow the below steps:

1. Once seed pods start to form, pick one now and then to check on their maturity. The best time to harvest the seeds is when the seeds inside the pod start turning brown. Picking them when the pod is completely dry and brittle might result in a lot of seed loss (since they will break open at the slightest touch, spilling seeds everywhere).
2. Take seed pods from every plant you have (and grow as much variety as possible) to retain genetic diversity. Allow the seed pods to dry out completely after you've harvested them. You can break open the pods with little effort when they're brittle. Winnow the seeds to separate them from the trash and debris.
3. You need more than air-drying brassica seeds if you're planning on saving these seeds for years. You can use rice cooked in the oven for 45 minutes or silica gel packets. Fill a glass container halfway with the baked (and cooled) rice or silica gel. Put the seeds in an old pair of stockings or

mesh fabric and secure them with a rubber band. Place the seeds in the glass jar and screw the lid on tightly.

4. Leave the seeds in the air-tight glass jar with the rice or silica gel for at least two weeks. This process will cause the seeds to enter dormancy entirely and last for years.

5. After two weeks of drying, you can remove the seeds and store them in another labeled container or Ziploc bag with the rest of your seeds.

Remember, all brassicas can cross-pollinate, so if you're growing spinach and broccoli in the same garden, you'll need to be careful since most brassicas are also self-incompatible and require polli-nators. The easiest way around this is to grow only one brassica variety (only spinach, broccoli, etc.) and rotate the array of brassica every year (grow spinach this year and broccoli next year, for example).

Under the proper conditions, you can keep most brassica seeds for five years.

Alliums

Alliums include all varieties of the onion family and garlic, chives, leeks, shallots, scallions, and spring onion. It is rare to find a hearty, savory dish that does not include some form of onion. Are they even more of a staple than potatoes? You're doing something wrong if you don't have "stinking lilies" in your garden. They're hardy, delicious, and easy to grow from saved seeds. Just as is the case with the brassica family tree, the method of harvesting seeds from alliums of any variety is pretty much the same across the board:

1. Alliums will flower in late spring. The bulbous flower stalks will tower over the foliage. The best time to harvest alliums is generally on the cusp of fall when the flower heads wither and turn brown.
2. Once the flowers start to brown, you can collect the seeds by cutting the flower stalks and shaking them into a bag or container. You may need to use your fingers to dislodge some of the seeds gently.
3. Dry your onion seeds like any other: Spread them thinly on a paper towel (or mesh screen) and let them dry for one to two weeks until they pass the fingernail test.
4. Remember to store and label them correctly.

Keep in mind that all species of alliums can cross-pollinate. Alliums are self-compatible (but they do require pollinators). This classification means that you can grow more than one species in your garden, given that you take the proper precautions to prevent cross-pollination. You'll have to pollinate them manually.

Allium seeds don't have a long shelf-life at all, with the germination rates declining by as much as 50% every year they're kept in storage. Don't plan on storing allium seeds for more than a year for best results.

Potatoes

Whether baked, fried, or mashed, there's a way to enjoy this starchy, blank canvas root vegetable for even the most picky of eaters. Potatoes flower and produce seeds in fruit that look like tiny tomatoes, but in many cases, potato flowers dry out and fall off before they have fruit with seeds (in colder climates, the potato "berries" are more likely to develop). The most popular way to

grow potatoes is from "seed potatoes," which are just regular potatoes you plan to use as "seeds" next year.

Growing potatoes from seed requires a few steps:

1. Collect the berries and carefully mash them in a bowl to
   not damage the seeds. Add water and allow the concoction
   to ferment in a warm area for five days, stirring it at least
   once daily. Pulp will float to the top, and seeds will float to
   the bottom.
2. Pour off the floating pulp, strain the seeds, and rinse well.
   Spread the potato seeds onto a tray with parchment paper
   or paper towels.
3. Let the seeds dry for one to two weeks or until they pass
   the fingernail test—label and store in an air-tight
   container.

Alternatively, to grow potatoes from potatoes, follow the steps
below.

Store-bought potatoes are covered in chemicals to prevent sprouting, so growing potatoes from them is not advisable. Instead, buy
potato seeds from the start and save seed potatoes from the
resulting yield. Here's how to grow potatoes from potatoes:

1. Choose potatoes to use as seed potatoes next year. Brush
   the soil and dirt off, but do not wash them; doing so may
   result in premature sprouting.
2. Storage conditions for seed potatoes are essential. Store
   them in a dark, cool area (below 50°F) and away from
   other vegetables and fruit. They will likely start to sprout
   within a few months regardless, but keeping the
   temperature and conditions consistent will prevent this
   from happening for as long as possible.

3. You can plant small potatoes whole, but you can cut larger potatoes into pieces as long as you ensure at least two or three "eyes" on each piece.

The downside to growing potatoes from seed potatoes is you can only store them briefly. It would be best if you planted them the following season; otherwise, the potatoes will rot. However, the seeds retain a high germination percentage for up to five years.

Carrots

Carrots are root vegetables and biennials, meaning they'll only produce flowers and seeds in the second year. To save seeds from carrots, you must sacrifice some of this year's yield and leave them in the ground until they flower and produce seeds next year. Luckily, waiting patiently for carrot seeds to form is, quite frankly, the hardest part of the entire process:

1. Leave the flower heads to ripen and mature on the plant until they dry out and turn brown.
2. Cut the flower heads off and place them in a paper bag until the seeds have darkened and the plant material is dry and brittle. This process might take a couple of weeks.
3. Transfer everything to a plastic container with a lid and shake vigorously to release the seeds.
4. Winnow the seeds using your method of choice before labeling and storing them in their final containers and resting place.

If it's any consolation, carrot flowers are beautiful and attract various pollinators and predatory insects to your garden, which aids in the yield size of other fruits and vegetables as well as pest control.

The shelf-life of carrot seeds is three years.

Beetroot

While beetroot is primarily grown for its sweet and vibrant root, its foliage is also edible and packed with vitamins and nutrients. You can add it to salads, smoothies, and sauces or prepare them just like other leafy greens (by itself, steamed, or boiled). Beetroot is also a biennial like carrots, meaning you'll have to wait two years after your first sowing before you can harvest seeds from them.

1. Once the beetroot starts flowering in its second year, wait for the foliage to turn brown before cutting four inches off the top of the plant.
2. Store the browned foliage you cut off in a cool, dry place for a month to allow the seeds to ripen.
3. You'll need to thresh and winnow the seeds since they're attached to the dried foliage. You can do this step with your hands (while wearing protective gear) or by putting everything in a bag and pounding it to release the seeds. Be careful not to crush the seeds.
4. Once you've separated the trash and debris from the seeds, they can be stored.

Beetroot seeds are attractive because most varieties contain multi-germ seeds. One beetroot seed will result in two or more seedlings. It's advisable to thin out your sprouts and keep the ones growing with vigor.

You can store beetroot seeds for up to four years.

Legumes

Growing beans is easy—plant them! Okay, okay, there's a bit more to it, but not much, in all honesty. Beans are one of the most popular garden crops, right underneath tomatoes. They have been elevating stews and soups for many generations. They're nutritious, easy to grow, and nitrogen-fixers (meaning they're great for soil health). Whether you're growing beans, peas, or lentils, the process of harvesting and saving seeds is the same:

1. Leave the pods on the plant or vine until brown. If you shake the pod, you should hear the seeds rattling inside. This process might take a few weeks.
2. Remove the pods from the plant and allow them to dry in the pod (in a cool, dry, dark room) for two to three weeks.
3. Carefully break open the seed pods and store them in airtight containers. It might be worth adding some silica gel packets to the containers for extra security. Beans sprout very quickly at the slightest hint of moisture.

There have been instances where legumes have been stored and successfully germinated a millennium later. However, aiming to keep them for at most ten years is advisable.

HERBS

Leveling up a dish with fresh herbs or brewing medicinal tea with leaves plucked from your garden is a special feeling for every aspiring (and experienced) gardener. Many home gardeners start their journey with a herb or "kitchen" garden before it blossoms into a miniature version of a fruit and vegetable forest. Either way, most herbs are easy to grow and even more straightforward to harvest seeds from. Not only that, but many herbs have exceptional pest control characteristics, which make them perfect for intercropping.

Parsley

Parsley is easily one of the most common herbs grown in a home garden. And even though it's a biennial, it's well worth the extra effort. It can be used as a garnish or condiment, adding flavor to virtually any dish.

To save parsley seeds, you'll have to wait until its second year when it starts flowering. Then, follow these simple steps:

1. Wait until the flowers dry out on the plant and the seed heads darken.
2. Cut the seed heads off with a sharp pair of scissors or pruning shears.
3. Gently roll or rub the seed heads over a plate between your fingers. The seeds should fall out with little effort. Some dried plant debris might fall with the seeds, so you might also have to winnow them.
4. Allow the seeds to dry for another week or until they pass the fingernail test before storing them.

You can store parsley seeds for up to two years.

Basil

Having such a distinctive and unique taste and aroma would cause the basil to be a finicky herb to work with, but it's pretty popular. Like most other herbs, it can be the perfect garnish or addition to many dishes, but you can also use it as one of the main ingredients in pesto sauce.

In cooler climates, it's typically grown annually; in warmer climates, it's a hardy perennial. In either case, it blossoms and produces seeds yearly at the end of its growing season. Here's how you save their seeds:

1. Once the flowers are dried and spent, it's time for harvesting. Carefully cut the flowers and place them in a paper bag, allowing them to dry for a few more days.
2. Vigorously shake the paper bag containing the flower heads to release the tiny seeds. You can also use a rolling pin or a similar tool to break the flower heads open, but be careful not to use too much force or pressure so you don't damage the seeds.
3. Pour all the contents into a bowl or shallow tray and winnow out the trash and debris by gently blowing (use eye protection) until only the seeds are left.
4. Store the seeds.

Basil plants keep flies, gnats, and mosquitoes at bay, so keep them close to your kitchen windows to reduce flies in your home during the summer months.

You can store basil seeds for up to five years.

Rosemary

Rosemary is not only an excellent herb for cooking, but the bright blue-purple flowers and full foliage give them an ornamental function. However, compared to all other crops listed in this chapter, rosemary is at the bottom of the list regarding how easy it is to grow.

The seeds are slow to germinate, and you'll have to grow them indoors (under fluorescent lighting) at the start of winter to be able to transplant them in the spring. But because rosemary is a perennial, you only need to sow them once (or again when you want more). Whether you take on the challenge of growing them from seed or you bought a couple of rosemary seedlings from a nursery, harvesting the seeds isn't complicated at all:

1. At the end of the season, allow the flowers to wither and dry on the rosemary plant before carefully picking or cutting them off. Place the flowers in a paper bag.
2. Let the flowers dry in the paper bag for two to three weeks. Shake the bag to allow the seeds to dislodge from the flower heads.
3. Pour everything into a bowl and ensure all the seeds separate from the flowers by rubbing the flower heads between your fingers or palms.
4. Winnow out the trash and dry debris using your method of choice before properly storing and labeling the seeds.

Rosemary seeds will stay viable under the proper conditions for up to six years.

Oregano

Oregano is a part of the mint family and a hardy perennial that can withstand even the harshest winters with only a thick layer of mulch for protection. Harvesting oregano seeds is easy:

1. After the growing season, oregano plants will flower. After a couple of months, the flowers will brown and become brittle. Pick them at this point.
2. Once you've harvested the flowers, hang them upside down to dry for a few days. Use wire and string and keep a plate underneath to catch falling seeds.

3. After a few days have passed, flick the seed heads to release the seeds into a plate or tray. Pick or blow out any plant debris and let them dry until the seeds pass the fingernail test.
4. Store and label them.

Oregano seeds (along with mint seeds) will remain good to go for up to three years.

Mint

Versatile herbs for you, your kitchen, and garden mint are at the top of that list. Eating or drinking it as tea has plenty of health benefits, including improved digestion, brain function, immune system, and oral health. In the garden, it is low maintenance, attracts pollinators, and repels pests.

Mint is a perennial but has a reputation for being a weed. If left unchecked, mint *will* take over your garden. You won't need to save mint seeds for your own sake because they spread like wildfire. However, if you do want to keep the seeds for whatever reason, here's how you do it:

1. After the mint flowers wither, the seed pods will develop. Please wait for the seed pods to turn brown before picking them. You can keep them in a paper bag or spread them on a tray.
2. Let the seed pods dry for another two to three weeks before squeezing the seeds out of the pods.
3. After squeezing the seeds out, do a fingernail test to see whether they need more drying time. If they're not dry enough, let them dry for another week and repeat the test.
4. When the seeds are dry enough, label and store them.

Consider planting mints in containers instead of in the garden bed to keep mints in check. But even then, mint might still "jump the fence" and end up choking out your other plants, so be sure to keep an eye on them.

Chamomile

Chamomile is another herb with many benefits for your garden, cooking, and health. Most home permaculture gardeners grow chamomile for its natural pest-repelling properties and to brew their chamomile tea. Chamomile tea has many health benefits and is famously known for its calming properties. And when incorporated into baking (or infused with butter, milk, or oil), it adds a delicate floral taste.

However, if you want to harvest seeds, you'll have to leave some blossoms there when you gather the flowers for tea. Here's how you harvest chamomile seeds:

1. Keep an eye on the blossoms—the seeds will form in the flower's yellow center. The seeds are tiny, so be diligent.
2. Once the seeds start to separate from the flower easily, you can cut them and use your thumb to rub off the seeds gently into a container.
3. Spread the seeds on a tray with parchment paper or paper towels and dry them for at least a week or until they pass the fingernail test.
4. Label and store the seeds.

You can store chamomile seeds for four years.

FLOWERS

Unless you're only growing self-pollinating fruit and vegetable varieties (which is very restricting and dull), you need flowers in your garden. Flowers are essential for two reasons: they attract pollinators, which results in a more bountiful yield, and they attract predatory insects who feed on pests that invade and destroy your crops.

However, I also consider beauty a necessity if it's functional. I mean a non-invasive, non-competitive flower with a primary function that isn't just to look pretty. Flowers you should avoid are toxic or poisonous ones (such as belladonnas, castor beans, and daffodils) or ones that grow exceptionally fast—which also means they quickly deplete the water content and nutrients from the soil (like aloe, morning glory, and butterfly bush).

When growing flowers, you want the most "bang for your buck." You want something that is easy to grow and requires minimal maintenance. For that, perennials are your best bet. However, the annual flowers I included in this list are well-versed in re-sowing or self-sowing. If you let them do their thing and don't harvest all their seeds or cut every flower, I can guarantee they will drop some seeds and germinate again next year.

Even though you don't need to save seeds from perennial flowers for yourself (unless you're expanding your garden), they make perfect gifts to friends and family members. Alternatively, you can donate them.

Most annual flower seeds will retain high germination rates under proper storage conditions for three to four years, and perennial flower seeds are typically good for five to seven years.

Alyssum

Let's start with one of the annual flowers on this list. Unless you're in a warm climate, alyssums are annuals, meaning they need replanting yearly. And while that is an absolute pain, besides that, they require minimal effort to maintain, and they are a great addition to your garden. The pros outweigh the only con of having to replant them every year.

Alyssum is part of the mustard family and boasts white or purple (or light purple) flowers. The seeds look like flat disks that line the stem where the flowers are. To harvest the seeds, wait for the flowers to wither and follow these steps:

1. Keep a close eye on your alyssums. You might have to take a trip to your garden every day when trying to harvest enough of these seeds. Gently flick each stem (where a cluster of flowers used to be) over a bowl—the seeds that drop freely are mature enough to be harvested.
2. Make sure you separate each "session" of seed harvesting so they all dry thoroughly. For example, keep today's seeds on a paper plate (write the date on the plate) and use a fresh paper plate for tomorrow's collection. Following this step, you can ensure all the seeds dry thoroughly before storing them.
3. As each batch of seeds passes the fingernail test, pour them into a container. If you're putting all the seeds in one container, note the date range of when you collected the first batch of seeds to the last. For example, you might write "June 22 to July 30."

The seeds fall off easily and quickly, so the trick is to collect them before falling off themselves. The good news is that Alyssum self-sows very well, so they'll likely pop up again next year.

Lavender

Lavender is a must-have in your garden! It's low-maintenance and gorgeous. Besides looking great on the ground, you can also dry them and use them as decoration in your home or pick a fresh batch and place them in the bathroom when you shower (they're great in aromatherapy for headaches, anxiety, and chronic fatigue).

The seeds are pretty small, about half the size of sesame seeds, but they're black, which makes them much easier to spot (unless they're on the ground). Harvesting lavender seeds is super easy:

1. Please wait for the flowers to fade and the seed pods to form in their place. You'll also have to wait for these seed pods to dry out while attached to the plant. You know they're ready for harvest when the pods turn light brown or grey. The seeds are loose and may fly out when gently shaking the stem.
2. To collect the seeds, you can snip off the entire stem and tip them over into a bowl or tray, giving only a light shake to ensure any seeds that you may have trapped inside the pods are also released.
3. There might be minimal trash and debris amongst your seeds. If they bother you, you can winnow them by blowing into the tray or bowl until they're gone.
4. Dry the seeds the usual way (spread out in a tray on paper towels or parchment) until they pass the fingernail test and store them.

Lavender seeds need a few months of cold stratification, so move them to the fridge for two or three months before you grow them.

Coneflowers

There are many varieties of coneflowers, but the most popular coneflower to grow in your garden is Echinacea. Not only are they attractive to pollinators and drought-tolerant, but they're also great for your health. Echinacea tea can help alleviate cold and flu symptoms and boost your immune system so you recover quicker!

To make Echinacea tea at home, pick a few fresh flowers (dried flowers also work) and infuse them in hot water for about 10 minutes (add a few chamomile flowers or mint leaves for extra flavor). To harvest the seeds, follow these steps:

1. When the leaves dry out and fall off, you can cut the remaining part of the flower (the spiky center) and leave it to dry for a week or two on a tray or paper bag.
2. Once the flower heads are completely dry, the seeds should come off quickly when you rub your thumb over them. However, the seeds are pretty sharp and pointy, so wear gardening gloves during this part.
3. The seeds should be dry now, but you can do a fingernail test and leave them to dry for a few more days to be safe.

Borage

Another annual on this list is borage. It's an excellent bee attractor, making it a perfect companion for your open-pollinated crops. The flowers are either strikingly blue or white (depending on the variety) and edible, making them great for garnishing or decorating fruit salads, cakes, pies, and anything else.

You can plant borage with cucumbers, beans, squash, and tomatoes to enhance the flavor of these crops and enrich the soil with calcium and potassium. Borage is an annual, but just like Alyssum, it does a great job of self-sowing. But if you want to, harvesting the seeds is easy since they're large and unique (a small black or brown pod with grooves and a white "cap" on one end). To harvest borage seeds, perform the following steps:

1. At the end of the flowering season, the flower petals will fall off, and a seed head will form. If you were to open up one of the seed heads now, the seeds would be green, meaning they're not ready to be harvested yet. When you break open a seed head, harvest the seeds when they're black.
2. To harvest the seeds, you can hold the seed head over a container and knock the seeds out.
3. Dry the seeds for a few more days if they still need to pass the fingernail test before storing them.

Borage leaves and stems have fine, silver hair and contain silica, which can irritate one's skin. It's best to wear gardening gloves when handling borage or harvesting its seed.

Marigolds

Most marigold varieties are annuals, but you do get perennial marigolds, too, so if you want to go that route, you certainly can. However, it won't matter once you know how to save these seeds yourself. Marigold flowers and leaves are also edible and make great additions to salads.

The cheerful petals of a marigold flower close (forming the seed pod) and dry instead of falling off like other flowers. Aim to harvest the seed pods when the entire flower is dry and the base of the seed pod (closest to the stem) turns brown. Then, follow these steps:

1. Cut and collect as many seed pods as you would like.
2. Ready a tray lined with paper towels or parchment. You'll see little black and white spears. If the spears don't have a dark side, they're not mature enough yet, and you harvested them too soon. The achenes (or spears) are pointy, so watch out.
3. Discard as many dried seed pods and petals as possible and spread the spears on the lined tray. Let the seeds air dry for at least a week before storing them.

Yarrow

Yarrow is an attractive perennial that improves soil quality (by bringing nutrients to the surface) and structure (because of its robust root system). Yarrow attracts beneficial insects like wasps, ladybirds, and hoverflies that keep aphid populations in check. Many gardeners believe that the yarrow's scent is a pest repellent.

In addition, you can harvest yarrow leaves, stems, and flowers and steep them in water until the plant material breaks down. This process will cause the potassium, phosphorus, nitrogen, and other minerals to be released into the water, effectively making liquid fertilizer. However, you'll need to harvest plant material before they start to form seeds. Just leave enough flowers so you can harvest seeds from them as follows:

1. Wait until the flowers have withered and the seed heads start drying out. Then, cut the seed heads and store them

in a paper bag to finish drying (for at least two weeks or until the heads are completely dry and brittle).

2. Rub the seed heads between your fingers over a bowl to collect them. The seeds are black and tiny, so be careful not to spill them.

3. Winnow any debris by blowing gently into the container. Store the seeds in an airtight container.

Because yarrow seeds are so tiny, they can easily take over your garden bed, so you'll need to be more careful. An easy way to get around this possible problem is to use blossom bags after the petals fall off and the seed heads start to form to prevent as many seeds as possible from going rogue.

The Next Step

Seeds give us so much, and we have a duty to protect them. Take your seed-saving to the next level, and inspire a new reader to get started too!

Simply by sharing your honest opinion of this book and a little about what you've learned here, you'll show new readers the value of seed saving and point them in the direction of everything they need to get started.

Thank you so much for your support. When we work together, we can make a huge difference.

Scan the QR code below

CONCLUSION

Every crop type, species, and variety exists today because someone decided to store them and pass them on to the next generation. But the decline in diversity is due to our collective negligent, capitalistic, or perhaps ignorant mindset. Don't get me wrong, I'm not saying that you are personally responsible for the decline in plant diversity. However, you can be part of the solution.

Seed saving is rooted in sustainability and self-sufficiency, first and foremost. It's a more cost-efficient option than buying seeds year in and year out, and it gives you way more control over the type and quality of food you grow in your garden.

On top of that, with every generation, the quality and resilience of your crops improve because your plants adapt to the local environment and reserve beneficial traits as a result. They may even become pest and disease-resistant. This adaptation leads right into preserving plant species and genetics of certain varieties of crops, which we know is very important for the future of gardening (along with food security and the planet in general).

When you think about how evolution works, technically speaking, all crops are hybrid crops (even heirloom varieties). What I mean by this concept is that if you go back in time far enough, all animal and plant life on earth share a common ancestor, and through a mix of evolution, natural selection, and time, different "branches" started forming. But in the end, we all come from the same single-celled amoeba.

The difference is that heirloom varieties are tried and tested. They have become stable over an unfathomable amount of time and will produce the same results no matter how many times you save and replant the seeds. If you cross two different crop varieties, the seeds will not produce fruit or seeds that are "true to type" for many generations. This concept means that while any hybrid plant can become a stable heirloom variety, it will be challenging.

You don't have to own heirloom plants or seeds to be considered an avid seed saver, but they do have inherent value—more so to the environment and the preservation of genetic material than us. The point is that heirlooms are essential and valuable to the environment, and therefore, they should also be necessary to us.

When it comes down to it, the seed-saving process starts way before there are even seeds available for harvesting. A healthy garden means healthy seeds, so ensure you do what is necessary to keep your garden well cared for. Whether that process includes permaculture principles and techniques, managing diseases, pests, and all other gardening obstacles is essential.

The most important thing to ensure your seeds survive storage and retain as high of a germination rate as possible is the drying of the seeds and the storage conditions. It is nearly impossible to dry a seed too much, but not drying it enough can have devastating consequences like mold growth or premature sprouting (which can result in the loss of an entire batch of seeds).

Additionally, you can sum up the conditions in which you store the seeds in three words: cool, dark, and dry. However, the consistency of the conditions is critical. Severe fluctuations in temperature and humidity can lower germination rates rather rapidly or result in bacteria and mold growth and cause them to sprout in their containers. Sunlight can damage the seed, so you shouldn't dry seeds in direct sunlight.

For these reasons, you should continuously monitor and intermittently inspect your seeds' storage conditions. This process is especially so if you store your seeds in a fridge or freezer since losing electricity (for whatever reason) can affect the consistency of the storage conditions. You never know when a refrigerator or freezer runs out of gas, there's an issue with the wiring, or it just stops working.

Running a germination test at least once a year for seeds you plan to keep in storage for more than two years will provide you with valuable data. For example, it will tell you how quickly your seeds are declining. If last year's test was 80% and it dropped to 40% this year, it may indicate that your storage conditions aren't optimal or consistent (and need closer monitoring or an alternative approach).

As with all other things in life, seed saving will include a lot of trial and error—so try not to be discouraged when you fail immediately. You'll eventually know all the ins and outs and how to troubleshoot (or even prevent) seed-saving obstacles or issues.

If you keep this energy going and save seeds from your garden crops every year, before you know it, you'll have more seeds than you know what to do with. When that happens, you have a few options, such as donating them, swapping them, gifting them to friends and family members, or starting your seed bank. And with a little commitment and time, eventually, you'll have a collection of precious heirloom plants (which are so unique they have an entire chapter dedicated to them) in a resilient and thriving garden.

You'll never have to settle for store-bought seeds again because you now have the essential information on seed saving, which you can go back and reference at any point. Please put it to good use, gain first-hand experience, and get involved with the seed-saving community.

Seeds are tiny vessels of life, a symbol and architect of abundance and continuity. Let us protect and nurture their legacies and pay tribute to their profound connection to the past, present, and future. So here's to them! May there come a day when everyone appreciates and respects the continued promise of a bountiful yield that seeds deliver us with every season!

REFERENCES

20 Insightful and Inspiring Quotes About Sustainability. Jersey Girl Organics. Last modified March 29, 2022. https://www.jerseygirlorganics.co.nz/post/20-insightful-and-inspiring-quotes-about-sustainability

Adams, J. (2022, April 9). *How to harvest and save allium seeds.* Seed Saving Hub. https://howtosaveseeds.com/learn/save-allium-seeds/

All That Grows. (2023, August 21). *What are heirloom seeds?* https://www.allthat grows.in/blogs/posts/what-are-heirloom-seeds

Allaby, R. G., Stevens, C., Lucas, L., Maeda, O., & Fuller, D. Q. (2017). Geographic mosaics and changing rates of cereal domestication. *Philosophical Transactions of the Royal Society B: Biological Sciences, 372*(1735), 20160429. https://doi.org/10.1098/rstb.2016.0429

Andrychowicz, A. (2018, August 22). *How to collect lavender seeds from your garden.* Get Busy Gardening. https://getbusygardening.com/collect-lavender-seeds-garden/

ASerna. (2022, August 15). *Ways to garden sustainably and reduce your carbon footprint.* Vizcaya. https://vizcaya.org/posts/ways-to-garden-sustainably-and-reduce-your-carbon-footprint/

Balltech on Demand, & PanAmerican Seed. (n.d.). *Best practices for storing and handling seeds.* https://www.ballseed.com/documents/Seed-Storage-Best-Practices-BallSeed-TechOnDemand-PanAmericanSeed.pdf

Braun, M. (2023, April 25). *Gardening 101: Collecting yarrow seeds for A thriving garden.* Shuncy. https://shuncy.com/article/how-to-collect-yarrow-seeds

Castaldo, N. (2018, May 29). *How (and why) to be a seed savior.* NRDC. https://www.nrdc.org/stories/how-and-why-be-seed-savior

Charbonneau, J. (2017, December 20). *The importance of heirloom seeds.* Southern Exposure Seed Exchange. https://blog.southernexposure.com/2017/12/the-importance-of-heirloom-seeds/

Charbonneau, J. (2020, May 6). *10 Reasons to save seed.* Southern Exposure Seed Exchange. https://blog.southernexposure.com/2020/05/10-reasons-to-save-seed/

Charbonneau, J. (2023a, March 31). *Saving seed: Ancient beginnings.* Southern Exposure Seed Exchange. https://blog.southernexposure.com/2023/03/saving-seed-ancient-beginnings/

Charbonneau, J. (2023b, May 2). *Top 10 tips for growing heirloom vegetables.* Southern

Exposure Seed Exchange. https://blog.southernexposure.com/2023/05/top-10-tips-for-growing-heirloom-vegetables/

Charland, D. (2014, September 16). *Seed preservation methods for home or community garden*. Connecting Communities to the Land. https://seewhatgrows.org/seed-preservation-methods-home-community-garden/

Chatterjee, R. (2013, May 13). *Why humans took up farming: They like to own stuff*. NPR. https://www.npr.org/sections/thesalt/2013/05/13/183710778/why-humans-took-up-farming-they-like-to-own-stuff

Chelsea Green Publishing. (2023, February 27). *8 Seed-saving myths*. https://www.chelseagreen.com/2023/eight-seed-saving-myths/

Cohen, B. (2021, June 8). *Why seed saving is important, for the plants and ourselves*. Grit. https://www.grit.com/farm-and-garden/do-it-yourself/saving-our-seeds-saving-ourselves-zm0z21jazbut/

Courtney. (2021, August 3). *How to save parsley seed*. The Kitchen Garten. https://thekitchengarten.com/how-to-save-parsley-seed/

Crossley, H. (2023, August 10). *How to harvest coneflower seeds – for more fabulous flowers next year*. Homes And Gardens. https://www.homesandgardens.com/gardens/how-to-harvest-coneflower-seeds

David, L. (2023, August 18). *Why heirloom seeds matter*. Food Print. https://foodprint.org/blog/heirloom-seeds/

Dian. (2022, December 22). *Rosemary: Everything you need to know*. Learning to Grow Our Own Food. https://dianfarmer.com/rosemary-how-to-propagate/

DLF. (n.d.). *Seed storage*. DLF Pick Seed. https://www.dlfpickseed.com/ag/technical-information/seed-storage

Dowell, T. (2015, February 4). *Seed saving law: What farmers need to know*. Texas Agriculture Law. https://agrilife.org/texasaglaw/2015/02/04/seed-saving-law-what-farmers-need-to-know/

Espace Pour La Vie. (n.d.). *Tips for harvesting self-fertile vegetable seeds*. https://espacepourlavie.ca/en/tips-harvesting-self-fertile-vegetable-seeds#:

Farmer Jer. (2023, May 30). *How to harvest and store oregano seeds ~ farmer jer's gardening*. Farmer Jer. https://farmerjer.com/how-to-harvest-and-store-oregano-seeds/

Fast Company. (2012, May 11). *In 80 years, we lost 93% of variety in our food seeds*. Fast Company. https://www.fastcompany.com/1669753/infographic-in-80-years-we-lost-93-of-variety-in-our-food-seeds

Genova, A. (2020, December 28). Seed saving movement calls for seeds to be publicly owned. *The Guardian*. https://www.theguardian.com/uk-news/2020/dec/28/seed-saving-movement-calls-for-seeds-to-be-publicly-owned

Grant, A. (n.d.-a). *Bean seed storage - learn how to save bean seeds*. Gardening Know

How. https://www.gardeningknowhow.com/edible/vegetables/beans/harvest ing-bean-seeds.htm

Grant, A. (n.d.-b). *Borage harvesting: How and when to harvest borage plants.* Gardening Know How. https://www.gardeningknowhow.com/edible/herbs/ borage/harvesting-borage-plants.htm

Grant, A. (n.d.-c). *Cucumber seed saving - how to harvest cucumber seeds.* Gardening Know How. https://www.gardeningknowhow.com/edible/vegetables/cucum ber/cucumber-seed-harvesting.htm

Grant, A. (n.d.-d). *What is true potato seed: Learn about potato seed growing.* Gardening Know How. https://www.gardeningknowhow.com/edible/vegetables/potato/ true-potato-seed-growing.htm

Grant, A. (2018, April 4). *Blueberry seed planting: Tips for growing blueberry seed.* Gardening Know How. https://www.gardeningknowhow.com/edible/fruits/ blueberries/blueberry-seed-planting.htm

Grant, A. (2021, April 26). *Heirloom vegetables - tips for growing heirloom plants.* Gardening Know How. https://www.gardeningknowhow.com/edible/vegeta bles/vgen/heirloom-vegetables.htm

Grant, A. (2022a, January 26). *Can I save seed potatoes for next year: How to save your own seed potatoes.* Gardening Know How. https://www.gardeningknowhow. com/edible/vegetables/potato/saving-seed-potatoes.htm

Grant, A. (2022b, April 18). *Pepper seed viability and storage - how to harvest pepper seeds.* Gardening Know How. https://www.gardeningknowhow.com/edible/ vegetables/pepper/harvesting-pepper-seeds.htm#:

Grant, A. (2023, March 27). *Can I harvest strawberry seeds - how to save strawberry seeds for planting.* Gardening Know How. https://www.gardeningknowhow. com/edible/fruits/strawberry/strawberry-seed-growing.htm

Grant, B. L. (n.d.-a). *Saving basil seed - how to harvest basil seeds from plants.* Gardening Know How. https://www.gardeningknowhow.com/edible/herbs/ basil/harvesting-basil-seeds.htm

Grant, B. L. (n.d.-b). *Saving tomato seeds – how to collect tomato seeds.* Gardening Know How. https://www.gardeningknowhow.com/edible/vegetables/tomato/ saving-tomato-seeds.htm

Hassani, N. J. M. (2018, July 2). *Seed storage - its importance and storage methods.* Forestrypedia. https://forestrypedia.com/seed-storage-its-importance-and- storage-methods/

Houzz. (n.d.). *Alyssum.* https://www.houzz.com/discussions/2150753/alyssum

Huffstetler, E. (2022, August 24). *How to harvest and save marigold seeds.* The Spruce. https://www.thespruce.com/how-to-save-marigold-seeds-1388591

Hughes, M. (2023, September 12). *Here's how to save seeds from your garden to plant next year*. Better Homes & Gardens. https://www.bhg.com/gardening/yard/garden-care/garden-seed-tips/

Jabbour, N. (2020, October 5). *Heirloom seeds: The ultimate guide to heirloom garden seeds*. Savvy Gardening. https://savvygardening.com/heirloom-seeds/

Jamie. (2023, January 25). *Wet vs. dry seed saving - complete guide for both methods*. Rennie Orchards. https://rennieorchards.com/wet-vs-dry-seed-saving/

Judd, A. (2022, January 14). *Seed storage & organization tips*. Growing in the Garden. https://growinginthegarden.com/seed-storage-organization-tips/

Learn Seed Saving. (2021, October 12). *Labeling, organizing, and inventorying*. https://www.learnseedsaving.com/labeling-organizing-inventorying/

Lee, M. (2015, May 11). *The value and significance of saving seeds and how it benefits you*. The Permaculture Research Institute. https://www.permaculturenews.org/2015/05/11/the-value-and-significance-of-saving-seeds-and-how-it-benefits-you/

Manner, L. (2020, September 11). *How the 12 principles of permaculture can transform your garden (and our world)*. Green Connect. https://green-connect.com.au/heres-your-guide-to-the-12-principles-of-permaculture/#:

MasterClass. (2021, June 7). *Types of seeds: Heirloom, hybrid, and open-pollinated seeds*. https://www.masterclass.com/articles/types-of-seeds-heirloom-hybrid-and-open-pollinated-seeds

Mathews, T. (n.d.). *Easy small scale grain threshing*. Permies. https://permies.com/t/28254/Easy-small-scale-grain-threshing

Meserole, C. (2022, September 3). *3 Mistakes beginners make saving seeds*. Grow Your Own Vegetables. https://growyourownvegetables.org/3-mistakes-beginners-make-seeds/

123Helpme. (n.d.). *Importance of seed storage*. https://www.123helpme.com/essay/Importance-Of-Seed-Storage-PC6869V826

Pavlis, R. (2018, December 25). *Germination test: How to test seeds for viability*. Garden Myths. https://www.gardenmyths.com/germination-test-seed-viability/

Pavlis, R. (2021, February 20). *Floating seeds in water - is this a good seed viability test?* Garden Myths. https://www.gardenmyths.com/floating-seeds-in-water/

Plastic What You Preach. (2019, October 11). *How to harvest borage seeds DIY*. Hometalk. https://www.hometalk.com/diy/grow/flowers/harvesting-borage-seeds-43861125

Rai, S., Kumar, A., Singh, I., & Singh, A. (2020). Seedborne diseases and its management. *Springer EBooks*, 611–626. https://doi.org/10.1007/978-981-15-4198-8_31

Real Seeds. (n.d.). *Saving brassica vegetable seed*. https://www.realseeds.co.uk/brassicaseedprocessing.html#:

Rhoades, H. (n.d.). *Saving pumpkin seeds: How to store pumpkin seed for planting*. Gardening Know How. https://www.gardeningknowhow.com/edible/vegeta bles/pumpkin/saving-pumpkin-seeds-how-to-store-pumpkin-seed-for-planting.htm

Rhoades, J. (2021, July 4). *How to save seeds from carrots*. Gardening Know How. https://www.gardeningknowhow.com/edible/vegetables/carrot/saving-carrot-seeds.htm#:

Sakawsky, A. (2020, February 12). *How to grow an heirloom vegetable garden*. The House and Homestead. https://thehouseandhomestead.com/heirloom-vegetable-garden/

Samuel. (2022, February 27). *How do you collect mint seeds*. Gardens Of Mine. https://gardensofmine.com/how-do-you-collect-mint-seeds/

Seed Savers. (n.d.). *Learn to save seeds: It's a winner!* https://seedsavers.net/why-save-seeds/benefits-of-seed-saving/

Seed Savers. (2014, September 30). *Tools of the trade: Our top 10 seed saving supplies*. Seed Savers Exchange Blog. https://blog.seedsavers.org/blog/top-10-seed-saving-supplies

Seed Savers Exchange. (n.d.). *Seed saving*. https://seedsavers.org/learn/seed-saving/

Seed Sheet. (n.d.). *How to hand pollinate - A beginner's guide*. Seedsheets. https://seed sheets.com/blogs/tips-and-tutorials/how-to-hand-pollinate

SIPA. (n.d.). *Is your seed protected?* Seed Innovation and Protection Alliance. https://www.seedipalliance.com/seed-innovation/is-your-seed-protected/

Smith, B. L. (2023, September 6). *Seed saving: The opportunities and challenges*. Edible Communities. https://www.ediblecommunities.com/edible-stories/seed-saving-the-opportunities-and-challenges/

Sow True Seed. (n.d.). *Planting guide and seed saving notes for beets*. https://sowtrue seed.com/pages/planting-guide-and-seed-saving-notes-for-beets#:

The Credible Hulk. (2015, July 8). *Genetically engineered crops and seed saving myths*. https://www.crediblehulk.org/index.php/2015/07/08/genetically-engineered-crops-and-seed-saving-myths/

Thorn, S. (n.d.). *Easiest and hardest seeds to save*. Permies. https://permies.com/t/134652/Easiest-Hardest-Seeds-Save

Van Druff, K. (2022, May 6). *How to harvest chamomile: Harvesting chamomile for tea & seeds*. Bunny's Garden. https://www.bunnysgarden.com/how-to-harvest-chamomile/

Van Eendenburg, H. (n.d.). *Seed saving at the front lines of the climate crisis*. Green America. https://greenamerica.org/story/seed-saving-front-lines-climate-crisis

Wikipedia. (2021, October 9). *Seed saving.* https://en.wikipedia.org/ wiki/Seed_saving

Wikipedia. (2023, October 11). *Heirloom plant.* https://en.wikipedia.org/ wiki/Heirloom_plant

Wildfong, B. (2016). *How to dry your seeds to perfection.* Seeds.ca. https://seeds.ca/ d/?t=09c1012100003118#:

Winger, J. (2018, January 23). *Where to buy heirloom seeds.* The Prairie Homestead. https://www.theprairiehomestead.com/2018/01/buy-heirloom-seeds.html

World Health Organization. (2018, May 9). *Mycotoxins.* https://www.who.int/ news-room/fact-sheets/detail/mycotoxins

www.ingramcontent.com/pod-product-compliance
Lightning Source LLC
Chambersburg PA
CBHW060938120626
46557CB00003B/1045